YOUR VOTE IS NOT ENOUGH

A Citizens' Charter to Make a Difference

Rajendra Pratap Gupta

SPEAKING TIGER

SPEAKING TIGER PUBLISHING PVT. LTD
4381/4, Ansari Road, Daryaganj
New Delhi 110002

ISBN: 978-93-88326-98-8
eISBN: 978-93-88326-99-5

10 9 8 7 6 5 4 3 2 1

Typeset in Sabon Roman by SŪRYA, New Delhi
Printed at Shree Maitrey Printech Pvt. Ltd., Noida

Rajendra Pratap Gupta has been involved in policy making for a decade and played a key role in drafting the policies enshrined in the election manifesto of the Bharatiya Janata Party in 2014. He is the founder of the Government Industry Dialogue, a unique platform to facilitate interaction between the government and other stakeholders. In 2009, he founded the Disease Management Association of India (DMAI), which was granted a special consultative status with the United Nations Economic and Social Council for its outstanding work. He is on the Expert Network of the World Economic Forum and has been an advisor to the Union Minister for Health and Family Welfare; he has also served as a member of the Education Policy Committee of the Ministry of Human Resource Development. As a member of the National Board for Khadi and Village Industries, he implemented innovative strategies to boost sales and profitability and also made systemic changes to root out corruption and inefficiencies.

Rajendra Pratap Gupta's first book, *Healthcare Reforms in India: Making Up for Lost Decades*, contained important prescriptions for reforms which are under implementation. He holds a bachelor's degree in science and social science, a master's degree in innovation and change management from the UK as well as short-term executive education from the Harvard Business School and Kellogg School of Management, USA.

PRAISE FOR *YOUR VOTE IS NOT ENOUGH*

'Rajendra played a key role in policy making in the most crucial of times by drafting the election manifesto of the BJP in 2014. His credentials as a policy maker are outstanding, and he is among India's foremost thinkers on economic policy and governance. In this book, he explains the role of citizens in policy making and implementation. He addresses in detail key issues facing the nation: among others, the creation of jobs, social security, and issues facing farmers and rural India. But, more than that, he also suggests solutions to the problems our nation faces. A must-read for every policy maker and every concerned citizen.' —Bhavna Vij Aurora, Political Editor, *Outlook*

'*In Your Vote Is Not Enough*, Rajendra has deftly addressed the most challenging issue facing the nation: job creation, and a major portion of the book is dedicated to it. I hope this will grab the attention of all readers. His innovative ideas on job creation, as well as those on a number of other topics, make this a vital book for all concerned about inclusive development. —Prabal Pratap Singh, Managing Editor, News18 India

'*Your Vote Is Not Enough* is unique in many ways and presents radical economic ideas. The author distinguishes between economic development and economic growth and makes a case for holistic development, and a bottom-up approach for building a new economic model. The suggestions in this book need careful examination and debate by policy makers and citizens alike. I am also sure that this book will help start a debate on the 'distributed growth model', which will help bridge the divide between the haves and have-nots and lead to job creation and sustainable development.' —Yatish Yadav, Firstpost

'We keep complaining that we have a broken system and the wrong policies, and we assume that our duty is only limited to voting and we cannot do anything beyond that. After reading this book, one realizes that the work to bring about change starts much before voting and continues much after. This book will be interesting to anyone who aspires to see and bring about a change in the system. This book is a seminal treatise.' —Ajmer Singh, *The Economic Times*

'Rajendra is one of the finest thinkers of our times, known for his rigorous evidence-based research. His idea, the 'cost of job creation', quantifying the amount of money needed to create 1-1.2 crore jobs every year, show his clarity of thought and deep understanding of the challenges of a developing economy. His out-of-the-box recommendations are a manifesto for a "Better India" which, if implemented, will help build the India of our dreams.' —Subhabrata Guha, *The Times Of India*

Contents

Introduction

We all want India to be better in every way, but most of us do not know how—and where—to contribute to make that happen. The general perception, too, is that the current system works only for the well-connected, or the high and mighty. That you and I, the common man, have no say in anything and that we are never heard. That we are consigned to passively suffer the system even though we regularly participate in the system of governance as citizens who pay multiple taxes and vote in the elections. Yet the truth is that we accept the system with all its flaws, without active resistance, and the result is—suffering! However, the reality is, as much as we hate politics or politicians, we cannot avoid becoming involved in the electoral process that chooses the politicians who govern the country, decide policies and run the administration. You and I face the impact of our choices—action or inaction—every hour, every day.

We cannot sit back and think that the Almighty will change our situation. Nor can we keep waiting for others to act. And mere good wishes, good intentions and prayers won't help change the nation. It is my belief that simply casting our votes and thinking that our duty has ended is wrong. We must ensure that the right policies are in place for the nation's future. Our work starts much before we vote and continues much after the polls.

We must understand the power of the democratic system and the important role of the citizens in the government, which was perfectly articulated by Abraham Lincoln in his statement: 'government of the people, by the people and for the people'. In a vibrant democracy like India, every enlightened citizen has the power to contribute to and drive change. In fact, it would not be an exaggeration to say: '*We* are the policy makers.'

Over the past decade, I, as a common man, have pursued changes in policy and have been successful in effecting them and, based on my personal experience, I am firmly convinced that each one of us can impact national policies and even change them. As they say, every country has the government it deserves. We certainly deserve much better governments, and governance, and it is up to us to ensure that we get them.

At no other time in history has our world been in such an exciting phase, when everything needs to be transformed. Our generation is not only a bridge between a rich legacy and an exciting, fulfilled future, we also have the vital responsibility of leaving behind a wonderful country for the generations which are yet to come. We have clear choices before us: we can act, or we can lose this opportunity and be left with regrets.

Based on personal experience, having played an important role in drafting two election manifestos and a few national policies, what I am writing in *Your Vote is Not Enough* is proven, time-tested and delivers results. This book is neutral, written from the perspective of a concerned citizen, and with no ideological bias whatsoever. This is my vision of what we, as citizens of conscience, must do and demand from our governments so that we may achieve what we were promised and what we so richly deserve.

With utmost care taken in quoting data, some purely for indicative purposes, this book delves in detail into the opportunities for job creation in different sectors, and provides a broad direction for key action areas like economic and social security, governance, and administrative reforms, amongst others. It lays out ideas about what we can do to actively participate in and change government systems and policies.

This book will help political parties arrive at a plan of action that is people centric and not just a political statement—to be forgotten after one election, and remembered again just before the next. I hope that this will spark a debate which will ensure that key points find place in the agendas of the major political parties and help citizens become active partners in policy making.

It is my hope that you will read these suggestions carefully, as initial thoughts intended to trigger wider debates among your friends, your communities and peers. It is my hope that you will be the harbinger of change.

Policies and How They Impact Us

Did you know that:

- India needs between 27,000–32,000 new jobs every day.[1]
- 69 per cent of jobs in India are under threat due to automation.[2]
- A child born in India today will be 56 percent less productive than she or he should be, when the child grows up.[3]
- We will lose much if we don't make amends to foreign direct investment (FDI) in retail policy and initiate programmes to support existing offline (mom-and-pop) stores. With Amazon buying stakes in Future Retail through the foreign portfolio investor (FPI) route[4] and 5 per cent equity in Shoppers Stop,[5] and planning to acquire Aditya Birla's More supermarkets with Samara Capital,[6] the war with mom-and-pop stores is certainly going to hit the businesses of small traders and create a divide in which the retail profits from India will go to two of the world's largest retailers, Amazon and Walmart, and, in the long run, we will pay a heavy price for it.
- With about 22,000 births and 8,000 deaths per day, we have a real challenge with 13,000 people being added to the population every day.[7]
- India reports the highest number of deaths of children in the world due to air pollution.[8]
- We are insured only up to a limit of Rs 1 lakh, no matter how much money we have in our bank

accounts.[9] Which means that we will lose all our money—other than the 1 lakh—should the bank fail and no one will be held accountable for our loss.

- Despite paying high taxes, we have no social security (pension, healthcare, housing), if we lose our jobs or once we retire.
- Out of a population of more than 130 crore, less than 10 per cent is driving the economy and benefiting from its growth and the remaining 90 per cent is struggling.

These are only some of the few worrisome facts about our daily lives in India. And almost all of them have come to pass because we, as citizens, have neither bothered to analyse the government's policies nor to question them. It is time that we woke up and involving ourselves in changing policies that don't work in our interest. This book might help us understand what our vote can do and the lasting impact it will have on the immediate, mid-term and long-term future of the nation. But the vote is not the starting point for change and the work starts much before we vote and continues until much later. Remember, most of the politicians are a product of the 'rigged' system and continue to serve and strengthen it. Politicians may change every five years, but the system continues. Of course there are exceptions, but they are few. So do we cast our vote and say that this is all that we can do and give up? Not at all.

Policy Making

A lot of times, people think that policy making is a complicated process. That the language in which policies are framed is either too technical or legal jargon that is difficult to understand. That it is meant for specialists. Further, a large number of us have come to believe that it is parliamentarians and bureaucrats who play an exclusive role in making policies. Yes, policies are made by bureaucrats and politicians, but if we write to them about our views on important topics, backed by logic, analogies, references and data, can they ignore us?

As a concerned citizen who has never accepted the status quo, I have always hoped to work to change the system for the better. I never had political connections and no deep pockets, the only thing I had was my passion and my first-hand experience of dealing with the system as a common man. It has certainly been a frustrating experience at every level.

Like everyone else, I have had to interface with government departments. I still do. Be it getting ration cards from the civil supplies office; my first driving licence from the road transport office (RTO); seeking healthcare for my sister, mother, brother and myself; securing electricity connections; opening and transferring my bank account; getting a PAN card; filing income tax returns, booking railway tickets online; opposing unethical practices within corporates; trying to get my rightful insurance claim; facing corruption in the police and consumer courts; even getting my PhD—every encounter with the 'system' has thrown up some challenge or the other. Never have I backed down. The fights were invariably long drawn out; I won most, some remained inconclusive, and some I lost. But with each experience my resolve strengthened. Then, in early 2000, I decided to change the 'system' and started writing to policy makers, law makers and anyone who mattered. After a few years, I put all of these accumulated thoughts and ideas in a booklet, *Truth Alone Triumphs*, and began sending it around to anyone and everyone who mattered. Some replied, and one person even wrote back, 'You must join the system to change it from within.' During the course of these interactions, I was invited by a leading politician to a meeting. Our meetings gradually increased and, in 2008, I was offered an opportunity to draft the manifesto of his political party. This was my first big success: from being a 'policy changer', I was offered a chance to try my hand at being a 'policy maker'. From time to time, I wrote on issues concerning the country's progress and the common man. My comments on various issues were sought by the Planning Commission, which was then the apex planning body of the Government of India, and even by multi-lateral agencies. A few of these communications appear at the end of this book, as proof that one can start driving change even as a common man.

In 2007, I quit my full-time role as the CEO with a large conglomerate and decided to pursue my interest on 'changing the system' and doing part-time roles to keep the kitchen fires burning. The journey so far has been nothing short of a roller coaster ride. I have played a key role in drafting policies for many sectors from 2014, including the National Health Policy 2017, the National Education Policy, policies and programmes for Building and Other Construction Workers (BOCWs), and the State Health Policy for Uttar Pradesh. It has been an exciting time. Some of the policies I have helped draft will impact this country for the next few decades and I can say with confidence that I have played a key role—even without a formal degree in public policy, and without being either a bureaucrat or a politician—in making things happen and you can do it as well. Globally, I have had the opportunity to work at the Global Agenda Council for the World Economic Forum in 2012–2014; I have worked in various committees and sessions of the World Health

Organization and the United Nations. On 14 November 2018, in my address at the Internet Governance Forum of the UNESCO in Paris, I requested the organization to focus on not just the proliferation of technology, and on productivity and profits, but also put people squarely in focus and create a roadmap to demonstrate the number of jobs technology and the internet will create in each sector, for a large country like India cannot afford to handle the threat to jobs which these twin modern phenomena pose.

We cannot afford to be silent spectators. If we have ideas which will bring about positive changes, we must chase them. Almost a decade ago, I started writing to the Ministry of Health with inputs on policy matters, and most of them have found their way into the policies of the nation. Of course, I cannot claim all the credit for myself; many other concerned citizens would also have written in. But I have played my part. On 19 October 2010, I received a letter from the Secretary, Government of Chhattisgarh, who found my suggestions helpful, stating that they would be incorporated in the future health plans of the state. On 9 February 2018, the Parliamentary Standing Committee on Health and Family Welfare asked for my inputs on the National Medical Commission Bill. In 2015–16, I had a chance to meet officials at the Prime Minister's Office and discuss some key reforms with them. After a few weeks, I wrote an email to a senior official, enquiring about the outcome of my meeting. The official responded, stating that the suggestions had been acted upon. When I found that an important suggestion regarding policies for women had not been included, I wrote to the Union Minister for Women and Child Development and the minister replied saying that it would be considered for inclusion when the policy was being revised. I was also nominated to the Global Agenda Council of the World Economic Forum and to the apex advisory body for healthcare in India (as a member of the Central Council for Health and Family Welfare of the Government of India).

The point I want to stress here is that all we need to do is to not sit idle but take up issues and make concrete suggestions. Trust me, responses will be forthcoming.

Policies Change When You Raise Your Voice

Now, let us examine a few policies proposed and withdrawn since 2014. This will provide us a sense of how big a gap exists between what a government wishes to do, how the bureaucracy interprets and implements those decisions and, finally, what impact they have on the population. While this list is by no means exhaustive, nor is it intended to castigate any government, the fact is that when the government does not get the right feedback and inputs, on time, bills and notifications are poorly drafted; this leads to the withdrawal of bills, circulars and notifications, or forces a sudden change in rules, which ultimately causes inconvenience to people like you and me. It is needless to mention that we are in part responsible for this by not being proactive enough in offering our suggestions. In the absence of the right suggestions, the following bills, ordinances and notifications had to be withdrawn.

- An ordinance to the Land Acquisition Bill 2013, which asked for some key amendments, had to be withdrawn. It was finally decided that the ordinance would be allowed to lapse.[10]
- In 2016, the proposal to tax the Employees' Provident Fund had to be withdrawn immediately after the budget announcement.[11]

- In 2016, again, the government, under pressure from trade unions, was forced to withdraw its proposed restriction on the complete withdrawal of the Provident Fund before the retirement age of fifty-eight years.[12]
- Following criticism over privacy issues, the draft encryption policy, which made the storage of all messages mandatory for ninety days, had to be withdrawn within twenty-four hours of being announced.[13]
- The government was forced to withdraw its circular directing technical colleges under the AICTE to observe Christmas as Good Governance Day.[14]
- A proposed excise duty on gold jewellery had to be rolled back.[15]
- A partial rollback in Railways passenger fares had to be undertaken soon after a hike was announced.[16]
- The Minimum Alternate Tax, levied on Foreign Institutional Investors (FIIs), was scheduled to be cancelled. However, under pressure from the tax department, the scrapping was stalled and the order modified.[17]
- The NDA government withdrew a ban on the sale of animals for slaughter in livestock markets across the country.[18]
- The government withdrew the proposal made by the Ministry of Information and Broadcasting to create a 'Social Media Communication Hub'. Petitioners had alleged before courts that this kind of hub could become a tool to monitor citizens' online activities.[19]
- The government issued more than 400 notifications, over 100 circulars and FAQs within the year that

> the GST was implemented. This was bound to cause undue harassment to citizens.[20]

These instances prove how important it is for all of us to study government notifications and policies, and if we find that they are not in the interest of citizens or consumers, or are against the national interest, we must put forth our views across to our local representative, or to the Central or the state government concerned, or even, if necessary, move court. There is no reason for us to wait until they have been proposed, or rolled out. Timely feedback will ensure that the correct policies, best suited to our interests, are created and implemented, and no time is wasted.

On the other hand, a number of inputs have also been provided by citizens, like you and I, on important bills concerning our future. Among the many bills that were put out in the public domain, for review, suggestions and feedback, the notable ones are: the Higher Education Commission of India Bill, proposed by the Ministry of Human Resource Development, which received 7,529 comments; the Draft National Health Policy, proposed by the Government of India in 2014, which received more than 5,000 suggestions; the National Policy for Women, which received upwards of 700 comments in 2016; the Insolvency and Bankruptcy Code Bill in 2015; the Real Estate Regulator Bill in 2016; the Draft Bill on Indian Institutes of Management in 2017; the National Medical Commission Bill in 2017; the Draft Model of the Goods and Services Tax Law in 2016; the return forms for the Goods and Services Tax in 2018; and the Data (Privacy and Protection) Bill in 2017 was put in the public domain seek for feedback.

The Process of Legislation

There are properly defined stages as a part of the legislative process for the passage of a bill in Parliament, and stakeholder consultation through public feedback is an integral part of the process.[21]

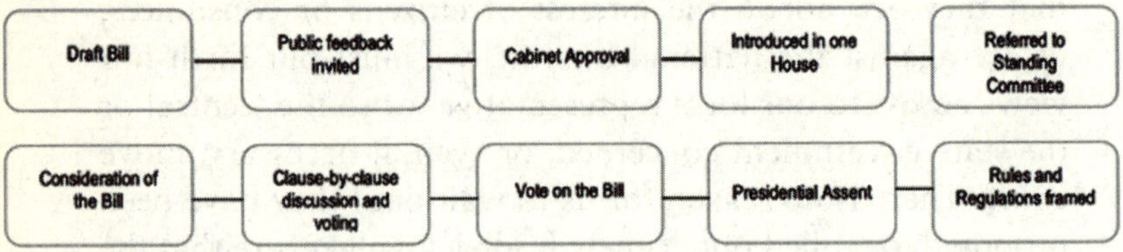

The question is, have we ever utilized this opportunity to give inputs to the government on important bills? If a nation of 130 crore-plus people gives only a few thousand suggestions, are we really serious about our own welfare? We must actively engage with all such issues that will affect us directly or indirectly.

In fact, for some of the key issues that we want to address, we should hold a small public referendum and send the report to the concerned authorities, and our local representatives. Every issue offers an opportunity, and we can thus contribute to policy making and reform.

Also, we must look at the new approaches and innovative ideas: for instance, the Ministry of Loneliness in the UK, and the Ministry of Happiness in Bhutan. It is the public which needs to come up with innovative ideas, and trust me, politicians love great ideas. So there is all the more reason why the citizens of the country must take a leading role in policy ideation and implementation. Lastly, planning is always worth when it is long term, it's the implementation which is short term. If the government of the day believes in seeking votes for delivery, and if voters like us are participative in the democratic process, there ideally should be no 'ribbon cuttings' or inaugurations in the government's last year in power, just before heading into elections. But the truth is that no matter which party is in power, the biggest and the best announcements happen in the election year or at around election time, and this clearly points to a flawed model, one which is based on lack of planning. Politicians must understand that the only goal of capturing power should be to empower people. And this understanding can come about only if citizens take active part in the reform process and question things that we cannot accept. It is wrong to think that one can simply vote and assume that the government of the day will take care of everything. A case in point: poverty did not engulf such a large part of the Indian population because generation after generation was born into poverty over the last seven decades. They were the result of year after year of poorly drafted and badly implemented policies. As citizens, we can aim to eliminate poverty in less than a decade by actively participating in governmental policies.

Our Role in Policy Making

The first step: Decide the issues that you stand for and will vote for

Every political party comes to prospective voters with an election manifesto which outlines its vision and commitments. To start with, we must send our inputs to the political party either over email or through letters or via its website, or in notes to representatives of the party, be they local, regional or national, to include the issues that we feel are important to the manifesto. Trust me, every political party wishes to meet the expectations of its electorate and be better than its competitor. In my experience as a policy maker over a decade, I have seen that political parties, ministries, and even bureaucrats, always go through important inputs, and if they feel that they are innovative or important, they will make it a part of their agenda and, at times, also reach out for further inputs.

In 2010, a member of the staff of a union minister called, requesting me to resend an email in which I had given them some inputs. My email had been deleted by mistake. I was later informed by one of the officers that the minister keenly read my emails, and would forward them to the bureaucrats in his ministry for action. I once received a call from the officer on special duty (OSD) to the Prime Minister, seeking inputs for the annual budget. Remember, ideas matter!

Think about the issues you are interested in, start putting your thoughts together, collate them, discuss them in your circles, and start writing. Conduct extensive research and include as much concrete data as possible. Remember, data and facts, especially if they come from people who are involved with issues at the ground level, are important. Try to be crisp, precise and constructive in your suggestions. This is important because, at senior levels, the demands on officials' time and priorities are many. More importantly, at least one follow up is vital.

I would like to offer one example of ground-level involvement. As a member of the National Education Policy Committee, I visited and met students across rural and urban India. Believe me, the best inputs for the education policy came from teachers, parents, and the students who attended classes between 8 to 12, not from the so-called experts in the education sector

Second step: Don't sit at home on voting day. You are the king-maker!

The best part about democracy is that every five years—sometimes even earlier—all elected representatives have to come to us for an evaluation of their work and seek re-election. It is entirely up to us to turn down their candidature, or give them another term. Many a time we despair, assume that our vote is immaterial, that the candidate's win is a certainty. These instances prove otherwise:

- In 1999, the Vajpayee government then in power had to face a no-confidence motion. It lost by a single vote.
- In the assembly elections held in Karnataka in 2004, R. Dhruvanarayan from the Santhemarahalli constituency polled 40,752 votes, while Krishnamurthy, his opponent, polled 40,751. Dhruvanarayan won with a difference of just one vote.
- In 2008, C.P. Joshi, then the chief of Congress, who was an aspirant for the post of the Chief Minister of Rajasthan, lost the Nathdwara seat to Kalyan Singh Chouhan by just one vote (62,216 to 62,215). Three people: his mother, his wife and his driver, abstained from voting. Had they cast their votes, he would have won by two votes. It is another matter, of course, that the election was later declared void for various reasons.
- In December 2018, the fate of six candidates in six gram panchayats in a panchayat election in the Barak Valley in Assam was decided by a toss of a coin as candidates tied with each other in the number of votes they polled. One vote each would have made all the difference.

Remember, it is finally our vote that gives us the authority, the right, and the opportunity to decide who wins! This poem perfectly captures the power of that vote.

The Power of One

One song can spark a moment,
One flower can wake a dream.

One tree can start a forest,
One bird can herald a spring.

One smile begins a friendship,
One handclasp lifts a soul.

One star can guide a ship at sea,
One word can frame the goal.

One vote can change a nation,
One sunbeam lights a room.

One candle wipes out darkness,
One laugh will conquer gloom.

One step must start each journey,
One word must start each prayer.

One hope will raise your spirits,
One touch can show you care.

One voice can speak with wisdom,
One heart can know what's true.

One life can make the difference,
You see, IT's UP TO YOU!
(Author Unknown)

If we do not exercise our right of franchise, we are as much at fault as the crooked politician who tricks voters. And, further, we now have NOTA (None of the Above) as a viable option. NOTA has been criticized for various reasons but, in my view, if a party loses an election because the option of NOTA was primarily exercised, the loss will ensure that the party chooses the right candidates. This happened in 2018, in the state elections of Madhya Pradesh, Chhattisgarh and Rajasthan. In Madhya Pradesh, a leading political party lost nearly a dozen seats where NOTA polled more than the victory margin and nearly twenty-two assembly seats were decided by a victory margin which was less than the number of votes polled under NOTA.[22] Surely such incidents will send signals to political parties that they are doing something wrong, that they need to make changes in the way they are conducting themselves.

Third step: Real policy work starts after the election, in the implementation of promises made

Once the election ends, leaders decide what they are going to deliver on the promises made before the election. So after the elected representative has settled down, it is our duty to remind him or her of the promises made in their manifestos and follow up on a regular basis. It goes without saying that many, if not all, of our elected representatives appreciate feedback on what they are doing and how they are doing it. Just a note of caution, which applies to all aspects of our lives including this: we must not be overly critical, we must keep our criticism constructive, and never forget to be factual, precise and soft in our writings.

The Guiding Principles of All Government Policies

All the policies, programmes, recommendations and actions of the government must compulsorily pass these filters. They must:

- Be citizen centric and improve the quality of their lives
- Lead to job creation and wealth generation—make India future ready
- Focus on quality, productivity and innovation
- Be eco-friendly, simple and hassle free

The government must proactively review all its working paraphernalia to ensure that the above overarching themes are embedded in every action of the government, so that people feel happy and proud of their country and the government and don't hesitate or cut corners in paying taxes, and can see the results in terms of delivery on ground. If India has to be a happy nation, it must put 'People above profit, welfare above wealth and trade over war'.

Policies That Will Drive India Beyond 2019 and Make It Future Ready

It is now important to get into specifics. In this chapter I have tried to cover as much ground as possible in terms of broad policy directions, and some suggestions might be provocative, but I am sure collective wisdom will lead to better ideas and suggestions. Also, this is just a template and a starting point, not limited to the next elections, but applicable to many more elections to come. These suggestions will help us step into the role of a policy maker and set in motion the processes to resolve the issues which we know need to be addressed. We will all see the difference which each of us can make if we proactively participate in these processes, and find that our elected leaders will not take us, our votes or suggestions for granted. Every five years, when we decide the future of our district, our state or the nation, we should also know why, and what for, we are making the decision to vote—is it the candidate we are supporting, the party or the ideology?

Jobs and Entrepreneurship

The ultimate result of right policies and good governance is a robust economy. The result of a robust economy is work for every hand, which is key for sustainable growth. If the country's citizens don't have purchasing power—which can only result from viable work opportunities—businesses cannot sustain themselves. Hence it is imperative that people either have jobs or enterprises to support their basic needs, or that the government supports them by providing social security. Also, while getting investments for 'Make in India' is not difficult, unless we enhance the buying power of Indians, we will not be able to sustain 'Make in India'. In fact, consumers are the real financiers for the investments in any sector by any company, as investors need consumers to buy their products. So the government's focus on attracting large-scale investments across sectors could be a misguided step, as what we actually need is to aim at creating not just large-scale enterprises, but also consumers on a large scale. Which means that the government of the day will have to ensure that population growth, economic growth, tax collection, income distribution and social security programmes are in sync with the dependency ratio—this ratio is a measure which shows the number of dependents, aged between zero and fourteen, as well as those over the age of sixty-five, to the total population segment aged between fifteen and sixty-four—and are mapped to resources. We need to factor in the dependency ratio to all our calculations else we will find it hard to take care of an ageing population.[23] Also, mapping resources with population projections will be important to set a time-bound target for population control and to achieve the desired population-replacement level. (The replacement level is the amount of fertility needed to keep the population the same from generation to generation. It refers to the total fertility rate that will result in a stable population, without it increasing or decreasing.)[24]

Given the protectionist policies being practised by nations across the globe, it is the need of the hour for us to formulate a plan to absorb members of the workforce who will be ousted from these protectionist economies. The day isn't far—some countries in the Middle East have already begun doing so, as has the US; many countries in the developed world will follow suit. Saving jobs is now a bigger challenge than creating jobs.

Also, according to McKinsey:[25]

- 60 per cent of all occupations have at least 30 per cent technically automatable activities
- Predictable physical activities have an 81 per cent potential for automation
- Data processing has a 69 per cent potential for automation
- Data collection data has a 64 per cent potential for automation

Automation is not a thing of the future. For instance, the Tata Motors' plant in Pune, which manufactured its latest model, the Harrier, has moved to a module in which over 90 per cent of the manufacturing process is automated.[26] There is certainly no exaggeration in the statement of Jim

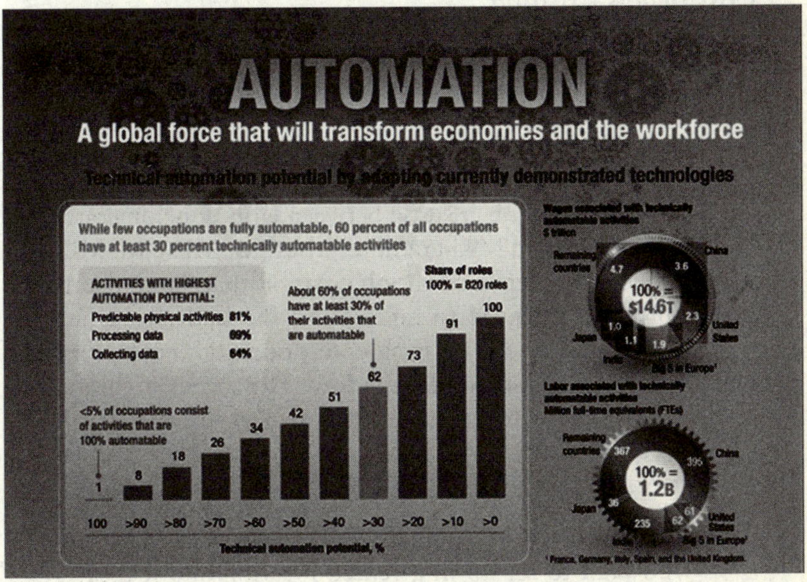

Yong Kim, then President of the World Bank, who said in 2016 that 69 per cent of jobs in India are under threat due to automation.[27]

Also, according to the World Bank, every percentage increase in GDP in India creates about 7.5 lakh new jobs.[28] So, for India to create between 1 crore–1.2 crore new jobs a year, the country needs to grow its GDP between 13.3 per cent to 16 per cent. The federal think tank of the government, the NITI Aayog, projects that the Indian economy will grow at an average rate of 8 per cent between 2018–2023.[29] This means jobs are going to be a perpetual problem.

It is my belief that there is an economic opportunity in every service opportunity. Each segment will create at least a million new jobs. We need to quantify them, provide investment, and support them through an enabling ecosystem.

Cost of Job Creation

We must also factor in one important input, the 'cost of job creation', an important economic factor which I have never come across in any deliberation on the economy or national planning. The cost of job creation can be calculated as the investment one makes to create a single job. If one were to compare the cost of job creation between large conglomerates and Micro, Small and Medium Enterprises (MSMEs), MSMEs will be much more efficient at job creation than large plants and industries. We need to understand the underlying fact that it is not just about creating enterprises, but enterprises where the cost of job creation is low. This needs a careful analysis for each sector and every segment of the industry. If we want quality jobs, we will have to work on this formula of 'cost of job creation and sustaining them'. For example:

- A restaurant in a middle-class town costs about Rs 20 lakh to set up in a rented location and it creates jobs for six people, so the cost of job creation is Rs 3.3 lakh.

- In a town like Aligarh, setting up a branded gift shop costs about Rs 45 lakh (15 lakh for the interiors and 30 lakh for buying stock) and it creates employment for six people, so the cost of job creation is Rs 7.5 lakh. A showroom for watches costs about Rs 1.50 crore to set up, and creates employment for six people, so the cost of job creation is Rs 25,00,000. A shop that sells flower bouquets costs about Rs 10 lakh and generates employment for three people, so the cost of job creation is Rs 3.3 lakh.
- Setting up a retail pharmacy in a small town costs about Rs 12 lakh and provides employment to four people, so the cost of job creation is Rs 3 lakh
- Setting up a typical village industry (small size) will cost about Rs 5 lakh, in addition to the cost of the land or rent. Such an industry will provide full-time employment to two people and the number of part-time workers may vary. Thus the cost of job creation is Rs 2.5 lakh.
- The investment required to buy a vehicle so that that it can be driven for an app-based ride-rental company is between Rs 4 lakh to Rs 7 lakh. If the vehicle is driven in two shifts, it can provide employment to two people, so cost of job creation is will range from Rs 2 lakh to Rs 3.5 lakh.
- A typical handicraft industry in a middle-class town costs about Rs 60 lakh to fund, which can create employment for twenty people. Thus the cost of job creation is about Rs 3 lakh.
- One needs a minimum investment of about Rs 30 lakh to set up a petrol pump, which creates about ten jobs. So, the cost of job creation is about Rs 3 lakh.

- In a rural area, it takes an investment of about Rs 3 crore to start 120 CSCs (Common Service Centres) which creates 120 entrepreneurs and fifty paid jobs. A total of 170 employees and entrepreneurs. So the cost of job creation on a PPP model in rural India is Rs 70,500.
- A sixty-bed cancer-care hospital in a tier-two town costs about Rs 40 crore to set up and creates employment for about 300 people. So the cost of job creation is about Rs 13.30 lakh.
- A mobile manufacturing factory needs an investment of Rs 800 crore (not factoring in the cost of the land) and will create 5,000 jobs, so the cost of job creation is Rs 16 lakh. This does not include the cost of the land.[30]
- A leading global manufacturer of mobile phones is investing Rs 4,915 crores and will create direct employment for 2,000 people, which means the cost of job creation is about Rs 2.5 crore.[31]
- A leading furniture giant has announced that it will invest Rs 5,000 crore to create 4,000 direct jobs in Uttar Pradesh.[32] There the cost of job creation is about Rs 1.25 crore.

Thus it is clear that larger the enterprise, higher the cost of job creation. We will not be able to address this important issue of job creation without factoring the cost of job creation. Also, here I have included only those businesses which will provide a minimum base income which corresponds at least to that of the lower middle class. There are, of course, occupations and vocations, like that of street vendors, in which the cost of job creation is even lower.

If we target the creation of 1 crore to 1.2 crore jobs per year, with a cost of 3 lakh per job, we will need an investment

Figures in crore	2016-17 Actuals	2017-18 Budget Estimates	2017-18 Revised Estimates	2018-19 Budget Estimates
Revenue Receipts	13,74,203	15,15,771	15,05,428	17,25,738
Capital Receipts**	6,00,991	6,30,964	7,12,322	7,16,475
Total Receipts	19,75,194	21,46,735	22,17,750	24,42,213
Total Expenditure	19,75,194	21,46,735	22,17,750	24,42,213
Revenue Deficit	3,16,381	3,21,163	4,38,877	4,16,034
Effective Revenue Deficit	1,50,648	1,25,813	2,49,632	2,20,689
Fiscal Deficit	5,35,618	5,46,531	5,94,849	6,24,276
Primary Deficit	54,904	23,453	64,006	48,481

** Excluding receipts under Market Stablisation Scheme

of between Rs 3 lakh crore and 3.6 lakh crore per year. This amount is very high considering that India's annual budget for 2018–19 was about Rs 24.42 lakh crore and we had a fiscal deficit of Rs 6.24 lakh crore,[33] in addition to the mounting debt, which has increased from Rs 54,90,763 crore to Rs 82,03,253 crore between June 2014 and September 2018[34]—a jump of about 50 per cent in just four years, and with electoral populism on the rise, the debt scenario is only going to worsen. (Refer to the table on p.31 for detailed estimates.)

Taking into account that every percentage increase in GDP in India creates about 7.5 lakh new jobs, we need an annual GDP growth of 13.3–16 per cent to create the number of jobs we need. But, at 7–8 per cent growth (which is the current growth rate and also the projected growth rate till 2022), we will create a maximum of 52.50 lakh to 60 lakh jobs a year and not the 1 or 1.2 crore jobs we need every year, and this means that the job deficit will add to the fiscal deficit. This twin deficit is going to create a serious social and economic challenge.

At the current rate of GDP growth, it is not possible to create the number of jobs the country needs and the government needs to plan carefully.

Also the overall, ongoing focus should be on quality job creation, so that individuals can take adequate care of the needs of their family, and save enough to live a comfortable life after retirement.

We need a multi-pronged approach for all this, and if that can be achieved, we will be able to convert our population into assets. The way forward in this is:

- People must see tangible benefits and must have a source of livelihood.
- Every adult citizen must mandatorily register on the

Population Portal (specially created for this purpose) with information about their employment status to avail the benefits of government schemes and for social security.

- Some sectors will undergo a transition and the policy makers and law makers have to carefully plan the transition for India's transformation. We have to identify the engines of growth and plan out implementation. These engines are: agriculture, services, MSME, R&D, education, health, tourism and defence.
- India will have to envision a 'domestic-population centric' economic scenario in which employment can be created to meet existing and urgent needs. Only then can we focus on catering to the needs of other markets (exports) and on the needs of travellers to India.
- Also, given a choice between large corporations and micro and small enterprises, we must always choose micro and small enterprises as the agents of massive job creation because the cost, per job, in the latter is much less and the potential for job creation much more.
- Automation will create jobs but will take away more jobs than it creates and, hence, we need to plan sectoral transitions carefully.
- Each segment will create at least a million new jobs. We need to quantify them, provide investment, and support them through an enabling ecosystem.

Here are some of the sectors in which opportunities and potential for job creation can be suitably tapped and exploited:

1. Agriculture: Agriculture remains the biggest employer in rural India and will be for the decades ahead. India cannot afford to transition its entire rural population to urban areas and agriculture should be an important focus area for the government. It must ensure irrigation, provide crop insurance and marketing support for agricultural produce. It must also guide farmers on crop rotation as well as the farming of herbs and other allied crops which will add to the farmers' income. Farmers must be trained and equipped with the skills necessary to avail all opportunities as they arise. In addition, rural areas need better infrastructure and connectivity, especially to towns nearest to them. Thus, rural India needs a different level of push in terms of connectivity, both in soft and hard infrastructure

Agricultural exports have tremendous potential to grow and create more jobs. At this time, we are looking at settling people from agriculture into other jobs, but what we need is just the opposite, for people to move back into agriculture, which is achievable with conducive policies.

Agriculture has a direct bearing on the health of the population. For instance, in tobacco farming. Given the challenges posed by tobacco production and consumption, and the cost to the economy which tobacco poses, in terms of the overall impact of health problems caused by tobacco consumption, the treatment of those problems, and the loss of productive lives, the government must formulate a comprehensive plan to curb the use of tobacco, and to transition tobacco growers to other crops, perhaps millets, herbs and other crops that suit the soil type ideal for tobacco, which will also provide equivalent returns to the farmers. Farmers, too, are willing to give up tobacco cultivation and transition to other profitable crops.

Ayurveda is India's gift to the world, and if India has

to be a global leader in traditional medicine, raw material for making herbal preparations must be made available. This needs a focussed approach. A few years ago, I held a discussion with the chairman of the world's top Ayurveda company, which is Indian. His biggest problem was the availability of raw materials. He was willing to sign a market-rate based forward contract with farmers (wherein his company was willing to pay prevailing market rates for the produce with a minimum guarantee on rate). Such contracts can lead to contract farming which will provide an assured income to farmers and also ensure that India remains the world's biggest supplier of traditional medicines.

Spice gardens in Goa; the famed coffee plantations of Coorg, where people can either stay inside the plantations, or nearby, and enjoy both the natural landscape and organic products—'agriculture tourism', a novel idea, has immense potential and must be explored.

We must envision a future in which farming is a profitable, secure activity, so that not only do the children of farmers continue their parents' vocation, other young people also view agriculture as a viable profession. We cannot afford to ignore the fact that profitable farming has the potential to create employment for 20 crore people.

Areas in agriculture where the opportunities lie:

- Food fortification
- Food processing
- Logistics; setting up warehouses and cold-storage facilities
- Developing and selling mechanized agricultural implements
- Crop insurance and bank loans especially adapted to rural realities
- Ensuring rural connectivity

- Apps and programmes to disseminate information; forecast weather
- Organic farming
- Irrigation
- Horticulture
- Sericulture
- Pisciculture
- Bee keeping
- Poultry farming
- Agri-tourism
- Weekend markets

2. Apparel: India is a vast country with enormous variations in topography and climate. Not only is it vast, the population is very large at 130-plus crores. Each part of India has different needs as far as clothing is concerned, and catering to these needs alone presents a massive opportunity to create new jobs. These opportunities range across different sectors: farming, to produce fibres such as cotton, jute and hemp as well as the plants used to make dyes; weaving, to produce hand-woven fabrics such as linen, wool and others; washing, both regular laundry and dry-cleaning businesses. And once the fabric is produced, there will also be a huge need for tailors and designers to produce the actual apparel.

The potential for the apparel business is naturally huge in the domestic sphere, but there is also an extensive global market that can be serviced.

There are also spin-off possibilities. For instance, used and leftover fabric can be repurposed into eco-friendly bags for daily use. We need to follow a regional cluster approach for this sector which could create employment for 5 crore people.

3. Healthcare: Good health for 130-plus crore Indians—our population alone presents one of the biggest opportunities in this sector. If we must keep our people fit, healthy and productive, in accordance with the principles of Universal Health, we need more medical professionals than ever: doctors, nurses, pharmacists, physiotherapists, psychologists, phlebotomists, counsellors, community health workers, lab technicians, fitness experts and coaches, as well as other trained technicians. There should be a surplus in the numbers of people we train so that we always have enough, even if some migrate abroad to meet the needs of the global health market.

The following key areas in healthcare need focussed analysis and development:

- Digital health, which will create multiple opportunities for jobs at the village and taluka levels, and boost the industries which manufacture and market medical devices.
- Health helplines, in different languages, which provide advice for acute ailments and medical emergencies so that people living in both urban and rural areas don't have to run from pillar to post trying to access a doctor. In cases of accidents and other emergencies, people should be able to avail first aid and urgent medical advice so that primary care can be given and lives saved. In some cases, patients should also be able to get prescriptions via phone for acute ailments.
- Hospices for the terminally ill, retirement homes for the elderly, and home-care facilities for the ageing are all areas which will need to be taken up with urgency given our population which is not only growing but also ageing.
- Similarly, there is a huge demand for child-care facilities of every kind.
- Medical devices and the IOT (Internet of Things) is another global opportunity for India in healthcare,

and, with the right infrastructure and schemes, India can break into the big league. India needs to set up at least eight special focus zones across the country for medical devices and health technology with the availability of requisite infrastructure and 'risk capital'. Capital alone will not help.

- Medical tourism is not only a big creator of employment, but also an effective earner of foreign exchange. If developed consciously and in a planned manner, this form of tourism will involve diverse, multiple industries: from publicity and advertising to insurance, quality control, technology of all kinds, human resources, travel and hospitality. The cascading effect of medical tourism as an industry has the ability to influence many others.

Healthcare has the potential to create employment for 4 crore people.[36]

4. Education: In terms of numbers, the Indian education sector is probably the largest in the world, with a network of about 14 lakh schools, more than 850 universities and about 40,000 institutes of higher education.[37] If we add the number of students in college to the 26 crore students in schools, the total goes up to more than 31.5 crore. If we add teachers to this number, it would bring the total number to more than 32.5 crore. Broadly, our education industry needs to serve a population larger than the population of the US. This segment needs to be looked at from the point of view of the economic value it creates in terms of jobs and taxes. Also, education is an insurance policy for the economic development and social progress of the country. This segment should be supported with clear policies as the highest priority. If this sector does not develop, India will fail to achieve its economic and social objectives.

Education has to move beyond books and classrooms and the focus should be on an application-oriented approach, not rote learning. More opportunities should be created by opening neighbourhood libraries, and science and computer clubs, which will not just get students moving towards science and technology, but also give an edge to India in terms of capitalizing on the educational and job creation infrastructure. We can learn from what Medellin, a city in Colombia, did by creating public libraries. I visited Medellin in 2017 and found public libraries in their metro stations from where people can borrow books and return them when they like. This public initiative has brought about a marked change in the people of Medellin, spurred by the habit of reading. We must replicate this, and on a much larger scale.

These are the key areas in the education segment which will benefit from investment and development:

- Training, employing and adequately compensating teachers so that more and more competent people are encouraged to take up the profession.
- Setting up and developing schools across the country with adequate infrastructure.
- Ensuring that schoolbooks have the most up to date and factually correct content.
- Developing and promoting the digital tools which aid and complement book learning.
- Conceptualize and create school stationery in formats and forms which will make learning enjoyable for students.
- Classroom activity needs to change from the lecture format to group-work setting.

- Setting up libraries across every district which will inculcate and encourage the habit of reading.
- Instituting Mathematics, Science and Computer Clubs (MSC clubs) in a neighbourhood cluster within a district so that more and more students become interested in these subjects.

The education sector has the potential to create employment for 2.5 crore people.

5. **Infrastructure:** In a country as vast as India, infrastructure is a sector second only to agriculture in its potential for job creation. It has an impact across sectors and a multiplier effect on many drivers of the economy, including banking, insurance and finance, besides the entire construction industry. One of the most surefire ways of boosting the country's economy, and of ensuring that it gallops along, is to devote focussed efforts to develop the country's infrastructure.

I will offer one anecdote, from personal experience, of how infrastructure, when managed properly, can not only provide value to citizens and consumers, but also ensure that no losses are incurred, either by the state or by individuals. A few years ago, I landed in New York in winter. All flights out of the city had been cancelled because of heavy snowfall. When I went to the airline counter to ask about my connecting flight to Washington, the attendant told me that while there was no connection available by air, he could, if I wanted, issue me a train ticket to Washington as the trains were running. I got my train ticket at the airport without any hassle and reached in time for my meeting in Washington. In London, too, I find that the Oyster Card, issued for use in the public transport system, works seamlessly across the train (tube) system and the bus service. Similarly, in Switzerland

and France, the travel card works seamlessly across trains, trams and buses. I am sure there are many more examples of such integration but these are the systems I have personally used and can vouch for. In India, where distances are large and travelling can take much time, all transport services—land, air and water—should be integrated and we could start with public transport. This will not be difficult, given India's competence and leadership in finding technology-driven solutions, and all bureaucratic hurdles which may arise in this matter must be addressed at the earliest.

The Railways owns prime land in every village and town across the country, and there are 7,349 railway stations (a number which does not include metro stations).[38] Each of these stations and metro stations can be converted into hubs for meeting points and for office space. This would make it most convenient for office goers and the youth. In a ripple effect, these hubs will encourage people to use public transport. Once feasibility studies are conducted for each location, commercial establishments such as restaurants, shopping malls and movie theatres could be leased on a monthly basis to generate revenue for the Railways, which will then be ploughed back into improving basic infrastructure.

Similarly, many busy roads are difficult to cross due to chaotic and high-speed traffic and this leads to accidents and deaths. The cost of building overbridges could be prohibitive due to the stretched budgets of municipal corporations. Therefore, it might be a good idea to lease the space on the sides of the overbridge for advertising so that the cost of construction can be recovered. This would work in both scenarios—in the case of structures built by municipal corporations or by private contractors on BOT basis.

These are the areas in India's infrastructure which will need focus to ensure sustained economic growth:

- Roads
- Electricity
- Water
- Air travel
- Waterways
- Railways
- Integrated transport services card
- Cement
- Painting
- BOCWs (Building and construction workers)
- Plumbing, carpentry, interior design and others.

This segment has the potential to employ 5 crore people.

6. Tourism: Boasting a natural diversity that ranges from high mountains and vast deserts to tropical forests, wide rivers and pristine seas, as well as a rich legacy of thousands of years of history, India presents a unique opportunity for commercial tourism, both domestic and foreign. Barring some instances, most tourism in India is conducted by the private sector. It is the government's responsibility to maintain natural assets, ensure the upkeep of monuments, build good roads and provide for electricity and drinking water. It must also ensure the safety of tourists. Partnerships between the government and the private sector to develop tourism should also be encouraged. For instance, the government could issue Tourism Bonds and raise money that would eventually be invested in the creation of tourism infrastructure across the country; also, the government could create a publicly listed entity, a Tourism and Travel Corporation, in which both the government and the private sector have equal stakes.

We must create a mobile application to ensure even better publicity for our tourist destinations. This application could feature attractions, ranking them on the basis of likes and tastes, including tips from and for travellers. This app could register—after due verification and for a fee—tourist guides, souvenir shops, cab drivers and others. The registration fee could then contribute towards the creation of a self-sustainable call centre dedicated to helping and guiding tourists. Not only would these initiatives help travellers, they hold the potential to becoming profitable on a standalone basis.

Geographical Indications (GIs) are internationally recognized signs that brand products which have a specific geographical origin, and possess qualities which are unique to them because of that origin. For instance, Darjeeling tea, Chanderi sarees and Alleppey coir. GIs offer a great avenue for the promotion of tourism as well as a sound business opportunity. India has 326 GIs across a range of products, and each GI can deliver outstanding business value even as they create a million jobs directly and indirectly. The government can work with the Quality Council of India and the Bureau of Indian Standards and work on a quality standard and a GI mark (along the lines of the ISI mark) to ensure authenticity. This can provide a boost to local producers, creating a source of income for lakhs and also become a source of foreign revenue.

India has a rich history and culture, and tourism can be built around themes, and tourist circuits developed with continuity in each theme. For instance, ancient cities with historic monuments, cities associated with the saints and other great people of India, cities associated with the freedom movement, among others. Varanasi and Madurai are among the oldest living cities in the world; they can be modelled and promoted along ancient themes without much structural modifications. These cities only need cleanliness and upkeep. The entire city of Ramnagar in Uttarakhand can be developed along the theme of the jungle—the famed Jim Corbett National Park is located in this city. Varanasi can be promoted for music, spirituality, yoga and education. Every city should come up with its own museum of history and every state or region should come up with the 'seven wonders' of its particular area. World-class convention centres, which can be used by the government as well as by corporates, can boost the economy of these cities.

I have already mentioned the coffee plantations of Coorg which have set up guesthouses for tourists; the Spice Garden Goa, the strawberry farms in Mahabaleshwar and Panchgani. These are excellent examples to emulate in the opening up of new avenues of agriculture tourism and will play an important role in boosting the profitability of farmers, agriculture, and the economy of rural India

Another great initiative would be to reclaim lakes and water bodies in our cities which can become magnets for local inhabitants as well as visitors to the city. The Ulsoor Lake in Bengaluru is a good example. It could be beautified, with a bridge providing a walkway over the lake, and a well-maintained and well-lit garden on its banks, with coffee shops and restaurants. Boats could provide joyrides upon the lake. Imagine the number of jobs these initiatives could create and, in a win-win situation, the money generated, from the entry fees as well as revenue-based contracts signed with various vendors and service providers, would lead to a healthy income.

National and wildlife parks are not only good ways to protect wildlife and endangered species, they can also be used to promote tourism with safaris and facilities for stay in guesthouses within the parks.

It is time that India promoted road trips, especially among its younger—and even older—citizens. These will support and create jobs in rural areas by the increased demand for restaurants, hotels and rest areas, and even integrated infrastructure such as travel plazas. This initiative could also result in the formation of biking and driving clubs across the country, which will not only help people, especially in urban areas, become familiar with rural areas, but also empower the economy of the countryside and support the creation of better infrastructure in rural and semi-urban areas

Imagine a souvenir shop in every major tourist destination. This can create a 'souvenir' industry worth crores of rupees. It is the government which should act as a facilitator in this, especially in providing the initial investment. The taxes which the government will earn from this venture will ensure that not only will it make up its initial investments, it will make money in the much longer term.

The overall employment by 2022 in the tourism industry (in hotels, restaurants and tour operators) is estimated to be about 7.2 million (72 lakh) persons. Segment-wise details are given below. This data only reflects human resource in the 'core tourism sectors'—hotels and restaurants, and tour operators.

Human Resource Requirements in Tourism Industry (in '000s)

	2008	2012	2018	2022
Hotels	1289	1869	2939	4065
Restaurants	2112	2481	2639	2834
Tour Operators	129	164	220	273
Total	3530	4514	5798	7172

Tourism has the potential to create value for 1 crore people. If we take into account the total number of jobs created by hospitality and travel, the figure could cross 5.2 crores.[39]

7. **Furniture Manufacturing:** Furniture is required for more than 25 crore households and 1 crore shops and offices across India. What we need is to ensure innovation and increased mechanization. There will be a positive impact on the timber industry as well and we will also have to take steps towards increasing the forest cover of the country so that the needs of all Indians are taken care of. This sector will create employment for plumbers, painters, designers and salespersons. This segment, with the potential for employing upwards of 30 lakh people, has immense scope for growth.

8. **Natural Cosmetics and Toiletries:** From time immemorial, India has had a rich tradition of creating and using natural aromas and fragrances, from sandalwood to essential oils. Given that a sizeable population of the country comprises the youth, and that there is a significant world market for perfumes, this segment presents a phenomenal economic opportunity. To make this segment the best in class in the world, what the country needs to do is to set up research facilities, validation and quality labs, as well as a robust marketing and advertising apparatus. This segment has the potential to create employment for 1 lakh people.

9. **Grooming and Personality Development:** India, with an average age of less than twenty-nine years, presents a significant opportunity for the services industry in the grooming space and India will be the world's biggest market for grooming and personality development services. Therefore, a natural corollary to the perfume industry is the grooming and personality development segment. This can be created by setting up a network of salons across the nation.

It is in this niche that the government should step into by creating the right programmes which can make India the global leader in the fields of cosmetics, beauty products and services, beauty and aesthetic dermatology tourism. These fields could become significantly bigger than health tourism in the next decade, given the right policies and promotion. India is famous for its rich herbal heritage and we must leverage and monetize it globally. This needs a clear vision, plan and a push, especially in facilitating comprehensive research and development, and the manufacturing of quality products. The Ministry of AYUSH (Ayurveda, Yoga and Naturopathy, Unani, Siddha and Homeopathy) should play a major role here. This sector can provide at least 25,000 jobs in each town and, in the bigger metro cities, the number of jobs created could grow to over 1,00,000. Overall, 30 lakh people could benefit from the systematized expansion of this segment.

10. Jewellery: The making of jewellery, as well as people's perennial impulse to buy, wear and invest in it, makes it a dynamic industry, rapidly changing, evergreen, and practically recession proof. Almost all Indian men and women are fond of jewellery and given the huge population of youth and the growing middle class, designing, cutting, polishing, and other activities, offers a major economic and a job-creation opportunity and currently employs 45 lakh people. If we do not get the policies in this segment right, we will lose the jobs to other countries. If the policies are pro-industry and pro-consumer, we can add at least 15 lakh jobs in this industry. This segment has the potential to grow immensely and support 50 lakh jobs.

11. Homecare Products for the Elderly: With over 13 crore senior citizens in the country, a number that is growing at 3 per cent per annum, this presents a great service and economic opportunity as a specialized segment. This must be a focussed opportunity from every aspect; be it food, clothing, tourism, medicines, technology, security, home-based delivery and care. Given the trend of nuclear families and the reality that children of today have less time and more money to take care of their parents, it makes sense to focus on this opportunity. 20 lakh people will benefit from the development of this segment.

12. Digital Infrastructure (Information Technology): With Digital India in focus, and stress laid upon it by the government, as well as the influence and impact of digitization in every facet of our life, there is great potential in the systematic development of this segment. The areas in which there is room for growth comprise the manufacturing of broadband devices, servicing and repairing devices already in use, the training and skill development of graphic designers as well as desktop publishing professionals, and the setting up and fine-tuning of Common Service Centres—the physical facilities which deliver the e-services of the Government of India to rural and remote locations where digital infrastructure is either negligible or absent. These centres, if scaled to every town and village, can create 50 lakh jobs and, more than just employment, they will make it easier for people to avail government schemes.

The Internet of Things (IOTs) is a growing industry, and India has to aim to be a global leader. India must target a minimum of 20 per cent of the global IOT market for products and services. All government certificates and registrations should move online and become Aadhaar linked. The ITES sector, if carefully groomed, has the potential to create employment for 70 lakh people.[40]

13. Computer Hardware: We require hardware—computers, mobiles, gaming consoles, printers, scanners, ink for printers, digital screens—for at least 25 crore households and over 1 crore offices and shops, in perpetuity. Therefore, this industry will be an ever-growing one. Given the proliferation of devices among a majority of India's population, the number of devices per capita is at least three, which means that, at any point in time, at least 500 crore devices are in use. While manufacturing is an obvious opportunity, there is tremendous scope in the sales and services as well as accessory markets, which will make this a matchless economic opportunity. Devices are upgraded frequently and, given the demand, this makes the industry recession proof. Also, what we need is a viable infrastructure for the disposal of electronic waste and this, in itself, will be a great economic opportunity.

This segment has the potential to create employment for 20 lakh people.

14. Software for the World: If we were to review the industry, where existing software provides continuing opportunities, but also in new and allied areas such as big data, automation, machine learning, gaming and others, the numbers are staggering. Given these numbers, India should retain its title of the being the 'software capital of the world'. India is the top IT destination across the world for information technology services and accounted for approximately 55 per cent market share of the US$ 185–190 billion global services-sourcing business in 2017–18.[41] However, moving on from that, we must also aim to create an operating system that is universal, user friendly and costs about USD 10. Another crucial area of improvement is in the setting up of software companies. We only have one company at the moment which is valued at USD 100 billion and we need ten more of them.

By creating more successful IT companies, we will create

the potential absorption of at least 20 lakh skilled people. This is crucial in view of the protectionist policies of the developed world. It is not enough for us to merely skill and upskill resources; we must stay ahead of the curve through innovation and expenditure in research and development.

15. Sales, Service and Marketing: India aims to become a manufacturing hub for the world. Specialized sales, service and marketing roles are required to support the various sectors. It is quite easy to create 10 lakh jobs in each sector.

16. Logistics: Comprising couriers, parcels and cargo services—even drones—to carry goods; and taxi services and bicycle rentals to transport people, the logistics sector presents a huge opportunity, especially in a vast and populous country like India. There are more than 80 lakh goods vehicles in the country and if we take an average of even two jobs per vehicle, a minimum of 1.6 crore jobs can come from this segment. If we were to add ancillary jobs in this segment, such as those of goods loaders, attendants at fuel stations, jobs provided by resting places on highways, the total number of jobs could exceed 2 crore.

17. Automobiles: India is aspiring to become a middle-class nation and we must factor in a need for an average of at least one vehicle (either two- or four-wheeler) per household, which translates into 2.5 crore vehicles. If we add the number of commercial vehicles, the number will go up by many factors. This massive industry needs to be supported by an innovative and enabling environment. The life of a vehicle should be capped at fifteen years and there should be lower taxes on buying a new vehicle to replace the old. This measure will further boost the automotive manufacturing sector, and increase its potential for employment. If life is made hassle-free for vehicle owners—by abolishing the interstate tax; by adopting the 'One Nation, One RTO' rule, as opposed to the present system in which each state has its own RTO; and by not levying tolls on highways—we will ensure that jobs are created for 20 lakh people in this sector.

18. Finance: The finance sector, with its wide-ranging ambit—banking, insurance, the stock exchange, bonds and funds—presents an exciting avenue for high-value job creation. With 100 crore people either invested in banks or being insured in some form or the other, and another 5 crore looking to invest either in bonds, or mutual funds, or in the stock markets, and with over 84 lakh people projected to be employed by the Banking, Financial Services and Insurance (BFSI) domain over the next couple of years, it will remain a great contributor to jobs.[42] This sector has potential to employ more than 84 lakh people.

19. Telecom and Mobile Communications: The sheer number of subscribers in the telecom sector is India's strength today but will not remain for long, unless the country develops and scales up communication technologies. The fact that Indian telecom companies have a debt of Rs 7 lakh crores, and gross annual revenues of about Rs 2.5 lakh crores, clearly proves that we have not addressed core issues in a holistic manner.[43] Put simply, the industry is gasping for breath. If this dire situation continues longer, there is more consolidation, pain and job losses in the offing. We need a transformation in the telecom sector and current policies are not sufficient to deliver it.

Indian brains are the best, and we must be technology leaders and technology suppliers to the world by 2030. For this, we need to invest in research, testing and development of futuristic communication technologies so that we don't become digitally enslaved to foreign technology. With over 100 crore mobile connections, and with both data and voice becoming affordable, to the extent that it is the cheapest in the world, India is poised for a massive boost in both the telecommunications and broadband sectors. This will mean a phenomenal opportunity to create and support jobs, including in retail, but it cannot be limited only to data and voice. We must expand the horizons of research and development, and it is here that the government and the private sector needs to work together. The policies of auction of telecom spectrum must be phased out and all allocation of spectrum in the future should be based on revenue sharing between the government and telecom companies. With gross annual revenues of the telecom industry at about Rs 2.5 lakh crore, even if the government auctioned or allocated the telecom spectrum for a small administrative fee, in addition to 40 per cent of the gross revenues, the government would be earning about Rs 1 lakh crore every year, an amount that would only grow. Most importantly, the telecom sector would not have been under debt servicing for having purchased airwaves. Lastly, despite 4G, due to the 'extortionist' policies applied by successive regimes, which appear short-sighted, we have not only killed the golden goose, customers are also facing an unacceptably low quality of voice and data service. It is time that the government of the day not only revisits all auction policies, but also converts them into a revenue-sharing model so that the government will have enough money from revenue sharing to pay for its expenses and address its perennial fiscal deficit problems.

Data privacy, data security and data handling need clear rules to protect the interest of Indian consumers. The US has the Patriot Act and the USA Freedom act; the European Union has the General Data Protection Regulation (GDPR)

Act; similarly, India needs to have stringent regulations with regards to data within its geography and of its residents. If data is the new oil, should we not proactively work to ensure that data is not only protected, but also retained in India? This has an economic opportunity for the country as well. The telecom sector, if carefully managed, has the potential to create employment for 30 lakh people.

20. Entertainment, Literature and the Arts: India is a young and intellectual nation. We are a knowledge economy, and entertainment and the arts will remain a big economic opportunity and a measure of a progressive society. We must set up centres of performing arts in every town, and hold regional literary, music and film festivals, so that local literature and cultures get a boost. More research is needed in traditional art forms and they must be promoted to keep the diversity of cultures alive and to also create fusion art forms and newer genres.

This will be a great economic opportunity for music and arts lovers as well as for those who manufacture the necessary instruments, besides other infrastructure that would be needed. Moreover, it will create at least a few thousand jobs in every town which will be supported by art lovers, and that is a big and a loyal segment.

India has a booming film industry and is the largest film producer with over 1,000 films made every year and about 1.5 crore people watch films every day.[44] This has a direct impact on job creation through artists, support staff, film theatres and associated services. These sectors have the potential to employ 40 lakh people.

21. Communication Skills: We have great thinkers in India, and we need great communicators. Almost all students, as well as professionals, need oratorical as well as other soft skills. We must invest in communication skills and in the psychology of behavioural change. These measures will contribute well to making citizens effective and create a few million jobs over the decade. More importantly, it will contribute to the development and image of our countrymen and the country. Though the resource pool for trainers will take from two to five years to create, once created, we will need a few hundred people in every town. A very good way to inculcate communication skills in the young is to institute children's parliaments in every school; this will not only make them aware of issues, their rights and responsibilities, but also make them articulate. These will help them to grow up into responsible citizens. This sector has the potential to absorb 10 lakh people.

22. Non-Governmental Organizations and Civil Society Organizations and Volunteers: Most Indians believe in helping and giving back, and in charity. This is not limited to financial contributions but also to physical efforts and time.

If worked on in an organized manner, high-school and college students, professionals and senior citizens could be invited to contribute to voluntary activities under the government's vision of public-private partnership for good governance. This group will become a major resource as 'first responders' for many schemes of the government. It is generally believed that NGOs, CSOs and volunteering is not a financially remunerative activity but, taken collectively, the administrative staff needed to support these organizations will become a big employer. Also, senior citizens and the Divyang who are fit and would like to keep active and contribute to the well-being of the society could find these ways best to give back to society, to remain relevant and perhaps even earn an honorarium. These sectors can easily take in 10 lakh individuals.

23. Retail: Goods in all sectors, from agriculture, consumer goods and healthcare, to education, technology and others, finally reach the consumer through retail channels and, hence, this sector is important for forward and backward linkages.

The government must focus on how to balance the big-box retailers and the 1.4 crore retailers and the families that they support. This industry is under serious threat from the larger formats of the retail and online marketplaces. The Indian online retail market—now mainly divided between two major players—is now in the hands of foreign retailers, and this is most likely a back-door entry for big-box retailers. These online retailers will buy out local supermarkets through the FPI (Foreign Portfolio Investor) route, or other indirect routes, and then lobby with the government to open 100 per cent FDI in retail. This is a reality in the making. India has to take care of small retailers to equip them with tools to withstand competition and stay afloat profitably.

One has to be very careful in assessing the role of foreign retailers. Let us understand one fact of any economy: retail expenditure is the means and measure of the wealth of the country. A major part of what you and I earn is spent on our daily needs (in consumption) and it goes out as retail spending. Ideally, this money should remain within our country. But with foreign retailers running the country's retail landscape, our country's wealth will now be repatriated back to the home country of these global retail giants. This is not something in India's interest or, to be blunt, in the interest of our national security. Moreover, the argument that these retailers will create millions of jobs is not true. With the level of automation that is happening, retail jobs will get squeezed, and for a country like India which needs 1–1.2 crore jobs a year, we will need to re-think our FDI in retail and online retail policy. This policy needs a recalibration.

FDI in retail must not be allowed beyond a minority stake at any point in time.

And if the government is not willing to roll back the FDI in retail, the fulfilment of retail orders must happen through existing local retailers, and a minimum of 70 per cent of the goods must be sourced locally. The consequence of not taking care of this could result in job wars, when the 1.4 crore retail establishments (and, by extension, the 7 crore individuals) find themselves out of employment. I have visited all major big-box retailers in the US, Europe, U.K. and the Middle East; they have the best of automation and employ the least number of human beings possible. So if we are dreaming of these retailers creating millions of jobs, we must rethink in the context of what they are doing in other parts of the world.

With a radical policy change, this sector can create employment for 5.6 crore people.[45]

24. Wholesale Trading: Between manufacturing and retail is wholesale and also, with the new trend of consumers going directly to the wholesale sector for their needs, the government will have to come up with guidelines so that both the wholesale and retail businesses are made secure with reasonable margins without impacting inflation. This is a more serious issue than the retail industry and we need to carefully draft policies so that retail jobs and opportunities are not threatened. We cannot blindly copy the Western models as those countries have populations that number only a few million, and have a much higher GDP per capita. We have to take care of the needs of a massive population, and that too with resources that are always stretched. Let's keep in mind one rule: FDI in retail will take away jobs from mom-and-pop stores while foreign wholesellers will take away the retail jobs. This sector has potential to create employment and jobs for 10 lakh people.

25. Packaging: We need packaging for everything in India—consumer goods, edibles, even agricultural produce. Therefore, packaging will always remain a key industry, especially for so large a population. And if we remain focussed on eco-friendly packaging, we could even serve global consumers. But first things first, the industry itself needs to innovate and transform. Plastic must be banned across the country in all forms of packaging. We need alternative forms of packaging, and since India is a world leader in jute and hand-woven materials, we must use this global opportunity and invest in the research, development and design of packaging materials. This sector also presents a special opportunity to involve differently abled and senior citizens. With concerted focus from the MSME ministry, the packaging sector has potential to be beneficial to 20 lakh people.

26. Village and District Haats/Weekend Markets: The concept of Farmers' Markets—better understood in India as village and town haats—organic markets and weekend markets need an institutional push to ensure that people have the means of selling their produce to mobile consumers and consumers from nearby towns.

With about 5.9 lakh villages and 7,900 towns in India, the idea of taking produce directly from the field to the consumer presents a significant economic and job opportunity for rural and semi-urban Indians.

This concept, to start with as weekend marts, will boost the travel and logistics industry, where a group of farmers go to the nearest neighbouring town and directly sell their product at city rates, thus increasing their profit. Also, upcountry people will travel towards the village haats or the weekend markets to buy the fresh produce. Moreover, this will lead to greater profits for the farmers. At least 10 lakh people will benefit from this push.

27. Aerospace and Defence: Our defence budget is now touching 3 lakh crore and that is a significant amount for a LMIC country. Despite the massive outlay, there is a shortage of up-to-date weaponry and resources for the upkeep and repair of existing weapons. It is high time that India looks to invest in cyber warfare and cutting-edge technology in the area of weapons. We have the most creative minds in the world, especially among the youth, and we must drive start-up efforts and innovations in this space.

Also, we must offer more to our soldiers in return for the valuable service they render on and within our borders, and in times of calamity. Every bus depot, train station and airport must have a best-in-class lounge facilities, complimentary, for soldiers and their dependents. This will also be a good way to convey our gratitude for what they do for us at the borders and within the nation and promote the profession. Needless to mention, they deserve much more as they risk their life and sacrifice their family life to protect our lives and our families. Defence and its associated sectors has the potential to create employment for 10 lakh people.

28. Skills Development and Training (Human Resources): To be competitive with the world's best, we need manpower that is best in class in all sectors. For that, our education system needs a massive overhaul in terms of competence, skills and employability. This is particularly important because today, on the one hand, we have an issue with job creation but, on the other, we are not able to find competent people to fill in the jobs. This has become a big challenge as a result of our education system, which has not only lost its relevance, but is in a shambles. Special skills development programs are needed for senior citizens. This sector can easily provide employment to 20 lakh teachers and people in other associated jobs.

29. The Food Industry: More than 50 per cent of the population of India is below the age of twenty-five and more than 65 per cent is below the age of thirty-five. It is expected that by 2020, the average age of an Indian will be twenty-nine years. Also, with a growing middle class, the parameters of affluence are being reinvented, with more and more people wearing designer brands, and dining out. We can safely assume that great numbers of people in India will eat out every day. This calls for a focus on this industry and its needs since this sector is a big employment generator—from chefs, waiters, bartenders, managers, security, and others.

Even if we only consider canteens in the education sector; there are about 15,22,346 schools, 39,071 colleges, 799 universities and 11,923 stand-alone institutions which add up to more than 15 lakh educational institutions.[46] If we assume that canteen facilities are made available in all institutions, we will create employment for 30 lakh people taking a low average of two employees per canteen. This number does not include government and privates offices; if we added them, this number would be double.

30. Hospitality: The youth is a major proportion of the Indian population and, with a growing middle class, we can expect a huge boost in travel and tourism, not only domestic but also abroad. While the youth should be in focus, we cannot also write off the 13 crore senior citizens and about 5 crore differently abled citizens. These segments will have a special interest in travel, if their needs are taken care of.

Every town should make plans for its own hospitality industry and to cater to this massive economic opportunity. India-wide, at least 10 lakh people can be absorbed into this sector.

31. Office Spaces: There is a growing demand for office spaces, especially with the enormous impetus given to the start-up ecosystem, and we need to be future ready in this area. We must focus on creating shared workspaces, meeting points and office-cum-cafés that gives people flexibility and cost-effectiveness. There is also a need to move from traditional workspaces and this represents a significant boost to transforming existing workspaces in terms of reorientation and redesign; a move that will only benefit all associated sectors. If planned and rolled out in every major city and town, this sector can absorb 10 lakh people.

32. Home Utilities: This category encompasses a wide variety of articles including household items, kitchen ware, gardening equipment and other gadgets. And with 25 crore households in India, the opportunity is in the 'essential growth sector'. If the government maintains focus on quality and innovation, we will be able to help improve both quality of life and productivity. We must recognize that women devote more time than men to household chores and a focus on utilities will directly empower them with more productive and better tools, so that they have to spend less time in chores.

As a corollary to the utilities sector, a 'support services' ecosystem, with house-helps, nannies and people providing support for other daily needs will be in itself another big opportunity for employment and entrepreneurship which could be reserved or promoted for women entrepreneurs. There is room for growth and value addition for 20 lakh people in this sector.

33. After Sales Service: Once sold, support is required for an entire gamut of products in the utility and technical sectors and even for furniture. Extended warranties, assembly facilities, demonstration and after sales service will create a massive economic opportunity for qualified and skilled individuals. The government will have to play the role of a catalyst to support this ecosystem through specialized skills development programmes in partnership with the relevant industries. Across the length and breadth of the country, 20 lakh people can be employed in the service segment.

34. Conferences and Conventions: An entire industry can be created around conferences and conventions. At present, India still does not have properly planned convention centres that can host, say, 25,000 people with the relevant infrastructure in their vicinities. In contrast, there are convention centres abroad which that can easily serve 50,000-plus people. It is time for us to identify towns, taking into account geography and climate, which can host large conferences, expositions and conventions. Once identified, not just the building of the physical structure is vital, but also the setting up of a supporting ecosystem and allied infrastructure such as hotels, tourism facilities, audio and video facilities, transport, and the manufacturing of conference kits, souvenirs and mementos. If well planned, a convention centre can be a major contributor to tourism and overall economy of a region.

Indian embassies abroad could act as major marketing arms to bid for major conferences, events and shows in India. These initiatives will need initial government support but will, within a decade, pay for themselves. In all, there is potential for 50 lakh people to be employed in this sector.

35. Sports: India is still not a sporting nation despite its huge youth potential. If sport as an industry, and a national culture, develops well, schools across India themselves present a massive opportunity. The areas in which the opportunities lie are infrastructure, coaching, the manufacturing of sports equipment and the staging of large and lucrative competitions.

The advantages of such a push are many. If developed as a culture, the country itself will become healthier and reduce our expenditure on healthcare. We will also emerge as a sporting nation with achievements in international meets and our medal tallies will enhance the soft power of the country. Sport, and all its allied industries, can easily put 10 lakh people on the road to jobs and prosperity.

36. Yoga, Meditation, Naturopathy and Spirituality: India is an ancient land which people have always visited in search of spirituality, meditation and yoga. This draw must be leveraged as a business opportunity and as a soft power for influence. And the earlier we do this, the better it is for us, before the West monopolizes the sector. We need trained human resources and centres across the nation to make this a 100-billion-dollar opportunity and a major tourist attraction for a world that is desperately seeking to connect with the inner self, and is looking for harmony and peace. We have an International Yoga Day, but we need to do more than just broadcast group yoga sessions on television. We need training centres, lecture series, and a well-organized advertising and marketing effort to take yoga to people all over the world. These should be our exports which will bring billions of dollars to the country. An interesting fact: the sales of yoga pants have surpassed the sales of jeans and has become a billion-dollar industry.[47] There are two vital points to note here. First, the segment is extremely lucrative and, second, we must exploit this segment before the West jumps on to the bandwagon. There are jobs for 20 lakh people in this sector.

37. Journalism and News: The consumption of news is growing across India over all media—in print, through voice, the internet and television. Given the enormous number of regions in the country, and regional dialects, the scope of growth appears phenomenal. In terms of direct employment, this sector has room for 1 lakh people. However, an additional 10 lakh jobs can be created indirectly through infrastructure—institutes which teach courses in journalism, in mainstream as well as regional languages, and train journalists, technicians and others.

38. Start-ups: As citizens of a predominantly farming nation, Indians are inherently entrepreneurs. For farmers are essentially start-up entrepreneurs. They prepare the ground, sow seeds, and wait for results that are dependent on many variable factors, and finally reap a harvest. As all start-up enterprises tend to be, farming is a very risky profession. Ideally, India should be the start-up capital of the world. Being an entrepreneur is in our DNA.

However, what we lack is an ecosystem that supports start-ups. We do have a programme called Startup India but it lacks an institutional setup and is managed by the same kind of bureaucrats who have been a major cause of the stalling of India's growth and hence the programme has not delivered on its goal. To ensure the success of Startup India we need a Startup Government, one that works like a startup and has a similar mindset.

What the government should ideally do is to set up a society along the lines of a India Startup Community Trust, on a PPP basis, wherein the government sets aside a fund of, say, Rs 10,000 crores, backed by some of the best entrepreneurs and investors in India on board as professionals. No bureaucrat, whether serving or retired, should be appointed in this entity. The government should stay at an arm's length to make the trust an independent body. This body can easily become the biggest wealth and employment generator for the government—in addition to creating opportunities for 10 lakh people.

39. Security and Surveillance Facilities for Offices and Residential Complexes: Technology has completely changed the dominant paradigms in the areas of security as well as surveillance. We must leverage the start-up community in this area to innovate and develop new avenues so that not only are our needs for security from external aggression, at the borders, taken care of but also internally, in our living spaces and day-to-day lives. For this, we need a vision and an action plan. Funding of Rs 25,000 crore will yield dividend in multiples in the near term with newer technologies being developed. What's more, we have the best resources in terms of manpower and I believe that our home-grown talents can give the biggest global defence, security and surveillance firms a run for their money and take the security of India to newer heights. Most importantly, this sector can create 2 lakh jobs per year directly and indirectly.

40. Panchayats, CSCs (Common Service Centres), At Home Entrepreneurs (AHE) and Allied Activities: According to the latest available data, there are about 2.5 lakh gram panchayats in India. There is tremendous potential to make these panchayats vibrant units for administration and job creation. Each panchayat should serve as a Village Administrative Unit (VAU) that looks after the sanitation of the village and the health, education and employment of the citizens it serves. The aim should be for villages, through VAUs, to professionalize their standard of delivery of services. If some villages are too small for VAUs, a cluster of villages could come together to implement and develop this model. Ultimately, a VAU, and the village it serves, will emerge as an independent economic unit. With so much potential for all-round involvement, this sector can directly employ 10 lakh people.

41. Public Utilities and Open Space Management: India is ramping up its road infrastructure, connecting a vast nation.

As more roads are built, people will be increasingly mobile. And increased mobility is crucial to the integration and integrity of the nation. The need of the hour is a network of public utilities which will make travel easier and more comfortable, and also contribute to a cleaner India. For instance, the Sulabh Toilet Complexes which have a network across the country. Multiple service providers, such as Sulabh, which have units every 10–25 kilometres can provide direct and sustainable employment to a significant number of people.

Another multiplier are complexes which provide facilities for shopping and resting, run by locals, every 50–100 kilometres on state and national highways. This in itself will become a major tourism initiative and create jobs locally in every cluster of villages, leading to millions of jobs nationally. These facilities can be geo-tagged and can provide all necessary facilities to long-distance travellers—fuel, motor repair, restaurants, local produce and products and facilities for layovers. This sector can employ 10 lakh people.

42. Festivals: India is a land of festivals which present a great opportunity for local and international tourism. Promoting festivals is an excellent way to get everyone to understand the cultural diversity of this great nation. The government, with the Ministries of Culture and Tourism working in tandem with state tourism departments, can fully support this initiative and create a new kind of tourism, festival tourism, to create opportunities for 10 lakh people.

The Kumbh Mela of 2019 in Prayagraj demonstrates the potential of festival tourism. With the government investing about Rs 4,200 crore, the Kumbh Mela is likely to generate a revenue of Rs 1.2 lakh crore and create 6 lakh jobs.[48] Similarly, we have other festivals such as the Pushkar Mela.

India is a land of festivals and festival tourism can boost the economy and create jobs.

43. Community Kitchens: A large working population, the increasing cost of living and the non-availability of nutritious food means that the government must become a facilitator in making life easier and healthier for people. India needs lakhs of community kitchens across urban and rural areas to provide tasty and nutritious food at economical rates; this is a big unmet need. These community kitchens, set up in urban, semi-urban and even rural areas will not only serve people but also create direct connections between farm and fork, with village cooperatives selling their produce directly to community kitchens. Including infrastructure, supply chain operatives, cooks, waiters, and other allied workers, we could create jobs for 10 lakh people in this model.

44. Police and Judiciary: The perception of the Indian police and judiciary among many is that they are not only incompetent and inefficient, but also insufficient in numbers. However, merely filling up vacancies will not help. In fact, if we continue under the current setup and mindset, any increase in the number of jobs will only lead to building upon legacy issues and will further deepen the malaise. Reforms in the judiciary and the police have been promised by every political party but none have succeeded for various reasons. It is now time to take bold decisions. In the final tally, it is the legislature which represents the will of the people and is accountable to them, so it must ensure that reforms are carried out according to the wishes of the people and the needs of our time. The effort to radically transform these twin arms of the Indian state to make them accountable and outcome driven must be accorded the highest priority.

However, before we even think of adding more jobs, we must consider a few reforms:

- Monetary fines for all defaults should be exemplary. This will accomplish two goals: firstly, the prospect of a huge financial outflow will in itself become a deterrent for defaulters; secondly, it will make the judiciary and police sustainable. For example, in August 2018, an outdated helpline number for Aadhaar made its way into the phonebooks of many cellphone users in an alarming breach of privacy. Google admitted that it was to blame for it.[49] While the company did own up, the breach raised several question: How did it really happen? Why did the company do it? Who gave it the authority? Why did the breach go unnoticed for as long as it did? And if a helpline number made its unauthorized way into our phonebooks today, what guarantee do we have that it won't happen again? It is quite possible that, tomorrow, someone could hack our phones in this same manner and leave behind incriminating data of any kind at all.

    The Telecom Regulatory Authority of India (TRAI) should have been booked by the courts, and its chief taken to task for failing his duty. Also, Google should have paid 5 per cent of its global revenues as a fine and its CEO should have been grilled by Indian law makers. Instead, this serious and potentially dangerous breach of privacy became big news for a few days and, then, everything simply blew over. Are we a banana republic that foreign entities can mess around with us and get away with it? India should learn from the GDPR of the European Union, where fines for breaches and non-compliance vary between 2–4 per cent of a company's global revenues.[50] India too must ensure that its citizens are not taken for granted. Also, such fines will help the country in continuing its investments in reforms and general administration, besides acting as a deterrent to defaulters.

- Promotions in the police and judiciary should not be based on age or seniority, but only on professional contribution and efficiency. The judge who delivers the maximum judgements per year, and whose judgements are not changed or reversed by other courts, should be elevated.
- Similarly, in the police, promotions should be based on the cases registered and solved and on how the public rates the police official who served them.
- It is quite shocking that people are lodged in jails for crimes, but on the tax-payer's money. This system must change and criminals must be made to pay for their incarceration, in the form of a fine. If they cannot afford the fine, they must work to make up for the cost of their stay, unless they are medically unfit.
- Police should be trained in soft skills, and if they fail to solve less than 80 per cent of the cases assigned to them, they should be transferred or demoted.
- Delivery of justice should be time-bound. Evidence is not created, nor are arguments a time-bound biological process. Judgements cannot be dragged for decades.
- Judges should not appoint judges. Appointments should be based on a comprehensive competency assessment exam like other services and, thereafter, all promotions should follow the standard assessment for professionalism and efficiency. The government or other judges should not be involved in appointments; this is important for the judiciary to maintain fairness and independence.

- All of these initiatives will mean the filling up of lakh of vacancies in the judiciary and the police, making them self-sustainable and independent on government funds. The common excuse is that we don't have resources to fund recruitment. That argument will not remain valid if we start charging higher fines. With more funds available, recruitment will become easier, and most importantly, people will regain trust in the system as crime and illegal practices come down drastically due to the time-bound delivery of justice.

With reforms, the police and the judiciary can potentially employ 2 lakh people.

45. Data, Research, Market Studies and Analysis: Looking for data in India is tougher than finding diamonds in coal mines. We face three challenges in data: integrity, integration and intelligence. Data is not available, and when available, it is not of acceptable accuracy. Or it is dated and old. Data authenticity is also a big challenge. India should reconsider the manual processes for the collection and updation of data and move to digital tools.

And when it comes to research, India, despite possessing the best resources in terms of intelligence, fails miserably. The average Indian student, and even the research community, does not have the aptitude for scientific writing and research due to the lack of an active and supportive infrastructure.

Future-proof sectoral growth can only happen if India becomes a world leader in research in all areas—be it the arts, humanities, technology or science. I am of the belief that the research community will have to be treated as a start-up community and supported institutionally. At the moment, our key research institutes are struggling to pay salaries; how can they focus on research and development?

This sector needs an investment of Rs 25,000 crores per year to come up with research that will make India the world leader in scientific discoveries and inventions which can be commercialized and which will pay for themselves. What we must do is to identify those sectors in which we want application-based research, and those which can be commercialized or licensed to industries.

These areas, taken together, can potentially employ 2 lakh people.

46. Scientific Research, R&D: Currently, India has about 2 lakh full-time researchers, and ranks below Chile, Kenya and Brazil in the density of its scientific workforce—calculated as one researcher per a workforce number of 10,000—and only 14 per cent of them are women.[51] India spends less than 1 percent of its GDP on research. Also, in terms of filing patents, while India files a comparably high number, it is the multinational companies which prove to be a major contributor to the total number.[52] More than 40 per cent of Indian researchers are working overseas.[53] We need to build a knowledge ecosystem which will lead to reverse brain drain. Considering that India has not won a single Nobel Prize in science after Independence, we must aim to have one Nobel laureate nomination every year, in one field or the other, from 2025. The quantum and quality of research must be high on the agenda, with a well-laid-out plan and investment. This must be reviewed at the highest level every six months.

India has to make academics more learning-based, more meaningful, and independent of tenure. I have met senior scientists in India who did not know what they were going to do after they retired or completed their tenure. If we cannot use our scientific resources wisely, we will be better off forgetting our dreams of becoming a global powerhouse. The country's investment in research must come from both the government and the private sector. Leading Indian companies must join hands with academic and research institutions to start research initiatives that can catapult India into becoming a research superpower.

With drastic changes in outlook and systems, we can easily create and sustain 1 lakh jobs in these sectors.

47. Senior Citizens: With a total number of 13 crore, this segment of the population constitutes a major consumer class. Personalized care, age-specific products, old-age homes and homes for the destitute all constitute major opportunities for job creation.

There is potential for providing specialized banking solutions to senior citizens too, especially since they depend on their savings, and the interest earned from the savings, for their livelihood. While it would be prudent to provide senior citizens an interest of at least 8 per cent, tax-free, investment schemes should also be innovated so that they can maximize their financial resources. India also needs to develop a special skills development programme aimed at benefiting senior citizens according to their age, health and education.

This sector can employ 10 lakh people across service categories.

48. An EWHR Agency: The basics of infrastructure, electricity, water, housing and roads (collectively called the EWHR), are important for every citizen, and for the country as a whole, and hence they cannot be executed, individually, either as mission mode projects or even as programmes. We have to go beyond them and create an institution, a EWHR Agency, in every state to monitor and implement the vision of the government to provide basic amenities to every Indian.

This institution should be constituted under an act of the Parliament so that it can be monitored at the highest levels on an ongoing basis.

These sectors, as a whole, create and sustain jobs for millions of people all over India and EWHRs can themselves easily employ 10 lakh people.

49. Night Shelters: The homeless number a few million in India. This population includes a significant migrant component, among them labourers who travel seasonally for work. The government must open night shelters in every city and every town for migrant workers and the homeless, with basic amenities for people. This is an initiative which the government must spearhead, both as a part of its commitment to ensure social security and as an avenue to greater job creation. These shelters can employ 1 lakh people.

50. Leather Goods and Footwear: A nation with a population of 130 crore needs leather goods: purses, apparel, shoes, slippers etc. If one was to factor in the potential for export, this number would rise, easily, to 150 crores. The magnitude of this industry and its impact on the economy can be imagined. What we need, however, is a focussed approach. With leather clusters in every state, and with technical and design institutes, we can make the sector a great job creator that can easily absorb 30 lakh people.

51. Tribal and Ethnic Heritage: A large percentage of the country's population, over 10.4 crore according to the 2011 census, are from tribal communities. Their traditional knowledge, products, designs and medicines constitute a great and distinctive heritage for our ancient country, and must be documented and promoted. These assets, properly packaged and marketed, will be in great demand, at home and abroad.

Not only will they earn the country revenue, but directly benefit tribal communities, the originator of these products as well as others connected with them. The total number of people who stand to benefit from these enterprises is 50 lakh.

52. The Specially Abled: The specially abled, divyang, in the country number 5 crore. While a niche market, the industry serving the specially abled is big enough to receive focussed attention from the government. Specialized products and professionals are required to cater to their needs. These products and health workers are needed not only for homes, but also in institutions. 10 lakh people can easily find employment in this sector.

53. Self-Help Groups: SHGs represent the power of communities. According to an estimate made by the NABARD, there are 22 lakh SHGs in India, representing 3.3 crore members. This can become a significant platform for entrepreneurship, especially among women. It is time that India focussed on this segment in a structured manner with specifically tailored schemes. This can be a major contributor to the economic upliftment of women in rural and semi-urban India, which is witnessing a decline in agricultural workforce and incomes. A multi-sectoral approach will take care of at least 5crore rural Indians and if applied to urban slums, the figure can cross 15 crore. Their contribution to making the economy sustainable can be well imagined. SHGs can create employment for 50 lakh people.

54. DEFA (District Employment and Entrepreneurship Facilitation Agency): Discussed in detail later in the book, the DEFA can be set up under the Ministry of MSME in partnership with the Ministry of Entrepreneurship and Skills Development in each district, with a presence in every town. This organization can partner, along with the Ministry of MSME, with business schools in the districts. Other professionals can also be hired from time to time or as needed. The role of the DEFA would be to conduct market studies, project consumption trends and market needs, what it will take for businesses to succeed, and to gauge the likelihood of their continued sustainability. Taken cumulatively over the 7,935 towns in India, DEFAs will create at least 10 lakh jobs.

55. Post Offices: 'India has the largest Postal Network in the world, with over 1, 54,882 Post Offices (as on 31.03.2014), of which 1, 39,182 (89.86%) are in the rural areas. At the time of independence, there were 23,344 Post Offices, which were primarily in urban areas. Thus, the network has registered a seven-fold growth since Independence, with the focus of this expansion primarily in rural areas. On an average, a Post Office serves an area of 21.22 Sq. Km and a population of 8221 people.'[54]

We are now setting up post office banks and this is a good step. Also, the network should be modernized with the upgradation of post offices and also expanding their scope of services and network. Each of these 1.54 lakh post offices can appoint extension agents who are paid a commission for the business they generate. These agents could be students or housewives or part-time professionals who can operate at large or from their own premises so that the services of the post offices are not confined to one building or office and are not limited by office hours. The employment thus created will not be a cost in terms of office infrastructure or salaries as they will be self-employed individuals who operate at their own cost and comfort. Post offices can create employment for 10 lakh people.

56. Khadi and Village Industries Commission (KVIC): The KVIC can create massive employment opportunities and lead to the creation of a distinctive economy based on give and take between urban and rural areas. The KVIC has between 8,000–12,000 outlets. If people were allowed to deposit, say, Rs 10,000 in outlets and take products worth Rs 12,500, they could go from door to door and sell these products as 'Khadi Ambassadors' or 'Khadi Mitras'. All profits accruing from the sales would be theirs to keep. The employment thus created will be at zero cost, in terms of office infrastructure or salaries, as these 'KVIC associates' will be self-employed individuals who operate at their own cost and comfort. On one side, KVIC will have zero investment to create this massive sales force, and on the other, it will create a massive outreach effort in the form of these sales people who will also make decent profits. We must open our minds to create new possibilities for income and jobs. This sector has the potential to employ 20 lakh people.

57. Multi-Level Marketing—Direct Selling Companies: This is a proven model for job and income creation and creates decent income opportunities for the middle class. Direct-selling companies currently employ 50 lakh people, and they have the potential to create 2 crore jobs by 2025.[55] The government must create an enabling ecosystem for such companies and also have a regulatory mechanism to ensure that products and services sold through such companies are of high quality, and also that consumers as well those people who are employed by such companies are not cheated. This sector has the potential to create employment for 20 crore people.

58. DEFA Business Representatives: These are a new cadre of self-employed people who could be trained in the laws of setting up an enterprise (for profit or not for profit) and also be entrusted with the compliance of those laws. Every district and every state can have such representatives who could work on a retainership with businesses. In terms of employment, this new sector could create jobs for 10 lakh people.

The total potential for job creation listed above adds up to over 78 crore jobs. This list is not exhaustive and, at the same time, there could be some overlap in terms of sectoral job creation, but there are many more segments and sectors which need to be planned and executed so that value can be added to the sectors and thus create more jobs. One thing is clear: we can create sufficient jobs to ensure that every household has one for its sustenance. We need to drill down sectoral job creation right down till the district and town levels and also factor the cost of job creation and how much the government has to invest in it.

So far, job creation has missed planning, mapping and institutionally supporting each segment and preparing them for the future and we are way off the mark when it comes to creating jobs. Even the government's think tank, the NITI Aayog, has not been able to connect GDP growth and its direct relation to job creation in terms of exact numbers. I could not find anywhere, either in government reports, or even a general statement somewhere, that India needs to grow between 13.3 to 16 per cent to create 1–1.2 crore jobs it needs every year. This is a glaring example of our faulty planning and also gives us a sense why the government is failing to create jobs.

We must converge all these job-creation opportunities under an overarching theme: 'Mission 250 Million Households', where the aim is to create employment for two people per household. We have to think of new possibilities from existing or new opportunities. We must also understand that jobs do not mean only salary-based and full-time services, they could also be commission-based and part-time. The primary goal in all our efforts should be that every household makes enough money to take care of its basic needs, with respect.

There will be transitions in the job market, that is certain. And if we do not periodically address these transitions, the transformation of the country will be painful. The need of the hour is a lean and flat institutional mechanism for each segment which will factor in transitions in each sector over the next decade, and on an ongoing basis, with the advent of technology and other developments, which will create a financial impact for the segment and an economic impact for the provider of services for that specific segment. We need an institutional mechanism at the Centre, in the states and in districts to use forecasting techniques for analysing and supporting segments as well as sectors for needs and reforms, and prepare them in advance.

Put simply, job creation is both the result and the cause of economic progress. Unless we understand this, we will create more anarchy and crime through unemployment. Agriculture and MSMEs hold the key for making the country recession proof and creating a robust economy which will lead to what I call a 'distributed growth' model. The current growth model we have is an 'accumulated growth' model where only large corporations are grossing billions and yet are consolidating through mergers and acquisitions and adopting automation, and thus reducing the job creation opportunities. We have a lot to learn from two nations: Germany and Australia. Germany's Mittelstand model, in which the state supports and encourages small and medium-sized enterprises run by owner-entrepreneurial families which put long-term profitability and sustainability above companies that are looking to create merely short-term shareholder value, is worth emulating. Australia, of course, remains unique in that it has grown without recession for twenty-seven years and remained untouched, not only by the Asian Crisis of 1997 but also by the global financial crisis of 2008.[56]

If India focusses on a sectoral approach, it can lead to double-digit growth in economic terms for the next few decades, provide livelihood for each household, social security for marginalized sections and boost savings rate to take care of old-age pensions and post-retirement expenses.

The Critical Sectors

In policy making, many of the sectors I have discussed in this chapter are referred to as the social sectors—ones with a social mandate or merely for public good. But to me, these are critical sectors and we undermine their importance by calling them social sectors. These sectors which play a vital role in providing a country with a distinct competitive advantage. To me, health and education are the most critical sectors which, if invested in adequately, can turn liabilities (large populations of developing countries) into assets and if ignored, transform the demographic dividend into a demographic disaster.

Health and Fitness—Creating Healthy Assets

Health is not just an issue of social mandate or social security, but also one of economic and national security. The Human Capital Index released by the World Bank in 2018 states that, 'A child born in India today will be 44 percent as productive when s/he grows up as s/he could be if s/he enjoyed complete education and full health.'[57] Poor health drastically reduces the productivity of people.

If people are physically and mentally fit, they are an asset; else they become a liability. Given India's vast population and the paucity of economic resources, it makes sense to examine our strengths, which are 1) no baggage to transition or undo as we are starting afresh 2) a huge proportion of the population being young 3) the heritage of Yoga and Ayurveda 4) that we have already begun our journey for universal health coverage with the Prime Minister's Jan Aarogya Yojana (PMJAY), the mega healthcare insurance scheme for more than 50 crore people.

In 2015, I wrote *Healthcare Reforms in India: Making up for the Lost Decades*, in which I stressed that healthcare should be a Unique Electoral Proposition (UEP). In a coincidence, the NDA government made healthcare an electoral issue by first launching the National Health Policy and then the PMJAY. But we still have a long way to go.

Firstly, we have to move away from a sick-care perspective. Our definition of healthcare should also include fitness trainers, yoga centres, cycling tracks, jogging tracks and swimming pools, besides hospitals and clinics. The Ministry of Health and Family Welfare must work with the Ministry of Urban Development to start opening up gyms, jogging and cycling tracks, swimming pools, Yoga centres etcetera in public parks. We must ensure that there are financial and employment incentives attached to fitness. For instance, people with health and fitness club memberships should get certain benefits and rebates in insurance premiums, as well as tax incentives. In a bold move, the retirement age of people with a demonstrated record of good health could be increased. Health and fitness guidelines must be developed for all age groups. Not only should they be promoted, but also enforced. Annual health-risk assessments through non-invasive and online tools should be made mandatory for all age groups.

Further,

- Instant point-of-care diagnostic tools should be promoted for instant health checks.
- Child health guidelines should be developed and promoted through the education system. A non-invasive annual health risk assessment, based on family history, diet, lifestyle and other factors should become an integral part of the education system. We must create a culture of fitness right from childhood.

Also, the portion of the GDP which we spend on the chronically sick are what I call 'negative rupees'. This money is spent on people who are chronically sick, or are either non-productive or are only marginally so. Therefore, prevention should be high priority, as the GDP spent on prevention are 'positive rupees'—they enhance the productivity of the workforce and give a positive return on investment.

- The National Institute of Nutrition should be tasked with creating a Recommended Dietary Allowance (RDA) for all age groups, based on calories as well as a balance of macro and micro nutrients. This will function as a guide to people on creating the ideal meal for themselves, based on their daily physical activity and must also be a part of all child health guidelines.
- All meals (packaged and served) should have calorific value and nutritional value mentioned explicitly, and those with less than 50 per cent of the RDA should have a clear identifying mark, so that consumers can make informed decisions about what, and how much, they should consume.
- Activity-based guidelines should be developed for all age groups.
- One Health Record (OHR): A single health record per individual, available for online access, should be made the norm. This should be provided by the government free of cost, and all healthcare providers, private and public, must be mandated to use it. This will go a long way in making healthcare accountable and outcome driven.
- We must stop following the ideas and diktats of the World Health Organization and indigenously develop our own models.

- Ancient India has always believed in 'food as medicine', and this proven concept must be documented by the government and promoted so that people eat right and exercise well. This will also be a good medium for projecting the 'soft power' of the country to the world.
- We must move our health and wellness centres from remote locations to shopping complexes and main market hubs so that people don't have to travel especially to these centres. Visits to these centres will then be part of regular market trips. The same must be done for rural areas, where village hubs should have health and wellness centres. It may make sense to start 'Janta Clinic' in every ward and block, which should have a doctor, nurse, a phlebotomist and a pharmacy to take care of all primary needs under one roof.
- India has a large population of the youth and the working-class, and it is imperative that we focus on occupational health guidelines for all age groups and sectors, and enforce them with incentives and disincentives.
- Since about 65 per cent of the Indian population is below thirty-five years in age,[58] it is important for the youth to invest in health savings accounts, which can be made tax-free or incentivized in other ways, and which can create a decent corpus for the government to invest in public healthcare facilities and also take care of the healthcare needs of senior citizens. This can be a viable funding model for healthcare, as long we can keep a replacement ratio of 2.1.
- The health of adolescent girls must be a specific focus area, something that should be conducted in a Mission Mode Programme.

- The Integrated Child Development Scheme (ICDS), which provides primary healthcare, preschool education and food to children aged six and under, should be moved from Ministry of Women and Child Development to the Ministry of Health and Family Welfare
- The Department of Pharmaceuticals must be moved from the Ministry of Chemicals and Fertilizers to the Ministry of Health and Family Welfare.
- Also, it is time to consider bringing health on to the Concurrent List of the Constitution. While the major healthcare schemes are being co-funded by the Centre and the states, most states do not demonstrate accountability in terms of delivery. This must be followed, in parallel, by a state-wide index of healthcare indicators and delivery so that the better performing states are rewarded.
- Public hospitals should be free for the poor, subsidized for the middle class and paid for by the well-to-dos. Why should the rich get free and subsidized services at premier government institutes? Also, doctors at public hospitals should be paid a fixed salary and a variable component should be added for outcomes.
- The OPD and IPD data available in public hospitals should be used to develop Artificial Intelligence-based diagnostic and treatment tools. This will go a long way in improving the quality of diagnostics and care.
- India is still dependent on China for Active Pharmaceutical Ingredients (APIs) used in the manufacture of drugs and this is a serious issue. India must ensure that there is enough capability in the Indian pharmaceutical sector so that we reduce our import of APIs from China to about 15 per cent or

less in the next five years. This needs the formation of a strategic vision and the tactical execution of a carefully drafted policy. The same approach is needed for medical devices.

- The IOT, which is coming up in a big way, must be leveraged in the healthcare sector.
- Families with an unwell senior citizen or a specially abled or mentally challenged member should get an additional tax relief on expenses incurred.
- A special mission mode programme is needed for senior citizens and people with co-morbidities.
- Healthcare delivery should be made tax-free in a real sense and, for that, all the products and services associated with healthcare should be placed under the zero-tax slab of the GST.
- Though the World Health Organization (WHO) has classified and included gaming as a 'disorder' (Gaming Disorder) In ICD-11;[59] but given the intense love for gaming amongst a growing section of children and the increased proliferation of digital devices and the internet, we must see this as an opportunity. I am firmly of the belief that though 'passive gaming' (sedentary gaming on devices) are certainly a cause of concern, but 'active gaming' (which leads to exertion or exercise) on devices, mixed with physical activity can help combat NCDs (non-communicable diseases) effectively and hence we need to create 'active gaming' tools for children and even for other age groups.
- Sri Lanka's healthcare spending is lesser than India in terms of GDP, and has much better health indicators and has successfully implemented a Universal Health Coverage scheme which is among the best in the region and, in some areas, better than Europe.

Also, even though it is a tropical country, Sri Lanka successfully eradicated malaria while India is still struggling to address the issue.[60] Thus Sri Lanka's model has some good examples for India to learn from, and must be studied and evaluated.

- The National Health Policy 2017 has suggested some radical changes and also added an implementation frame-work. The minutes of the implementation frame-work review meetings should be put in the public domain.

Education: The Key to Solving Major Challenges

In 2014, I was giving a talk in Singapore and had a chance to meet the Deputy Prime Minister of the country. He had made a great presentation in that conference, where he showed that Singapore, once a backward and small fishing village, had transformed into a First World Country in merely a few decades. I asked the minister what the one thing was which had contributed to this transformation. His response: 'Education'.

Education and economic growth are directly proportional. The Human Capital Index (2018) released by the World Bank states that, 'A child born in India today will be 44 per cent as productive when s/he grows up as s/he could be if s/he enjoyed complete education and full health.'[61] The poor quality of education drastically reduces the productivity of people. We need to address this as a high priority, if productivity and development are our goals.

Unfortunately, education in India takes the form of formal degrees, and that too through a rigid and closed system of schools, colleges and universities. Our country has had two National Education Policies so far; the first one in 1968 and the second in 1986, with a revision to the 1986 policy in 1992. India has not made great strides in education, and a long path lies ahead. Since the last policy, the world, and India, have gone through a dramatic change

In 1991, the country embraced globalization and liberalized the economy. In the last quarter of the century, we have passed through a churn which has impacted every stratum and sector of society. Information Communication Technologies (ICTs) have emerged as a new frontier in bringing about a paradigm shift. These massive changes have been denominated by enormous change in the population: from 83 crores in 1991 to 132 crores in 2017—there has been a 59 per cent increase in the overall population of the country. Along with the increase in population, the aspirations of citizens, too, have increased manifold.

The education system of the country must ensure that the potential of 70 crore youth, who comprise a significant part of the total, is maximized, leading to a prosperous economy. It must also ensure that it addresses the challenges arising out of the changing dependency ratio and socio-economic disparities to make India an inclusive society. The world confronts increasingly uncertain forces of change, and the youth of the country must be confident of finding a fulfilling livelihood and employment. Every single child must be assured of the acquiring the capacities and skills which will build the foundation for a good and productive life. Education will play a pivotal role and bring about a revolution in India's human development.

Every single young person in the country must have the opportunity to receive an education that equips her or him with the knowledge, skills, attitude and values that would make him or her a vital link in the transformation of India.

Education has to ensure that the country is prepared for the future. It should expand the horizons of thinking and transform every challenge into an opportunity. Education, not limited to academics, leads to the holistic development of the individual and contributes to the prosperity of the nation while retaining our traditional values.

For the education system to be more effective, it should:

- Move from being input to outcome oriented
- Shift from teaching to learning
- Change from rote learning to systems of knowledge transfer
- Become more application oriented than based on theoretical knowledge
- Lay stress on mastery of competence than on mastery of content
- Emphasize functional literacy over mere literacy
- Champion meritocracy over mediocrity

The population of the country is expected to reach 152 crores by 2030. More than 54 percent of India's total population is below twenty-five years of age. The average age of the population in India by 2020 is estimated to be twenty-nine years and the labour force is expected to increase by 32 per cent in India. In order to reap the demographic dividend which is expected to last for the next twenty-five years, it is essential that the youth in the country be equipped with civic spirit, along with employable skills and knowledge. For this, we need a revolutionary change in our entire education system.

India has accorded high priority to the task of fostering quality education and improving learning outcomes. This is in conformity with the emphasis of Sustainable Development Goals 4 (SDG 4) of the United Nations. But more should be done. We have glaring systemic gaps in the education system. Education has lost its purpose and direction, as large segments of the sector in India face a serious crisis of credibility in terms of the quality of education imparted and the employability of graduates produced. This is not just a moment of truth, but a call to action. Unless we transform the education system, we cannot transform India.

Reforms are needed in schools, skills development, education, higher education and research. These include major reforms in human resources for education, infrastructure and, most importantly, in the governance of educational institutions. The role of the community and the alumni in governance will bring about a major shift in accountability in educational institutions.

In my view, these are the crucial changes that are required:

- Students, in their earlier years, should not have the burden of school bags. They should be taught what can be observed, experimented or practised, with no books needed till Class 5
- No homework should be given
- Schools and educational systems should run from Monday to Friday and the weekend should be kept unoccupied for students at all levels
- The government could issue a mandate that textbooks should come in the form of files rather than bound books so that students can take out the respective chapters to be taught on each day for the class. This way, the load of schoolbags can be reduced by up to one-eighth. This can be done for notebooks too
- The teaching of history could be limited to regimes and rulers that brought in important changes and changed the course of history, or has an important lesson for the people of this generation. The mere memorization of dates doesn't serve much purpose

- All studies should be application oriented and not theoretical and a new pedagogy should be evolved for this
- The recruitment and training of teachers also needs to be based on newer tools, in keeping with the needs of the time
- The appointment of senior management, including heads of institutions, should be truly based on merit. A good step in this direction would be the creation of a state-level and national repository of human resources, ranked based on contributions to education and experience, in a transparent manner. All appointments made to institutions should be based on the merit list of this repository
- Also, it is time to ensure that, from Class 8 onwards, all students are compulsorily trained in some vocation
- Feedback from students and the overall results of the class they teach should feature in the assessment of teachers' performance
- We must institute part-time courses and online courses for all degrees. Education should be based on the principle of lifelong learning
- Education should be made tax free at all levels to reduce the burden on tax payers and knowledge seekers

Flexibility in the education system, without compromising on quality, is very important. If a student of arts in Class 10 wishes to pursue science in Class 12 or in college, the student should be given that opportunity based on a 'Competency Assessment Test'. We must remove artificial barriers in the education system and ensure that we produce the best thinkers and 'tinkerers' in all fields.

Much as it might gall us, had the current education system of India been prevalent in the world, none of the following scholars, scientists and researchers who shaped our thinking would ever have been possible. Charles Darwin, a sailor and a naturalist whose major research came from his five-year survey voyage around the world; George Johann Gregor Mendel, a monk who studied physics and mathematics, but whose path-breaking research in genetics came from his experiments in the monastery's garden; Louis Pasteur, who discovered the principles of vaccination, was an average student skilled at painting and drawing; he pursued Bachelor of Arts and Bachelor of Science degrees before completing his doctorate; Albert Einstein was trained as a teacher in physics and mathematics but was unable to find a teaching post and so accepted a position as a technical assistant in the Swiss Patent Office; most of his significant work was produced in his spare hours at the patent office; Friedrich August von Hayek, one of the most significant economists of the last century had doctorates in law and political science, and not economics; Kenneth Rogoff dropped out of school, went on to become a world-class chess player and is now a professor of economics at Harvard who served both at the International Monetary Fund and the Federal Reserve.

If all these great personalities had been tied up in a rigid educational system like India's, where cross-disciplinary movement is more or less impossible, they would have never done path-breaking work, but would have found a routine task commensurate with their qualifications and experience.

India is quite rigid when it comes to academics and research. We should remember that India has won only two Nobel Prizes; that too, before Independence: Rabindranath Tagore in the field of literature in 1913 and C.V. Raman in science in 1930. Clearly, post-Independence, the Indian education system has failed to make an impact on society and the world at large, in terms of new research and knowledge, and it requires a radical overhaul without delay. Our education system must embed flexibility of approach, blended with innovation and good governance, to transform this sector and this has to start at all levels simultaneously.

Research and Development

If India has to become a global leader in any sector, it needs to revamp infrastructure and invest resources in research and development. Public expenditure on research have been stagnant, between 0.6-0.7 percent of GDP, over the past two decades.[62] As per the latest Global Innovation Index, India is ranked 76 among 143 economies.[63] India will have to invest about 2 per cent of its GDP in research and development to attain a leadership position in at least a few important sectors such as industrial engineering (production process) and manufacturing (products), energy, pollution control, water, pharmaceuticals and defence. The key overarching themes of investments in research and development investments have to be the achieving of a leadership position in nanotechnology, in IOT, in Artificial Intelligence, telecom, genetics, agriculture and environment.

This calls for setting up specialized universities for each sector in every state so that the nation as a whole can join the movement. It seems to be the norm today that whenever we come up with a university, it is located in the borough of a powerful politician. This approach must change, we must locate our universities in areas where there are associated industries and nearby towns. Also, all universities must update their syllabi in engineering courses to stay in sync with the needs of industries. The syllabi is currently lagging behind by at least seven to ten years and is not in sync with the changing times. All academic research must be application-oriented and must ensure that India is future ready.

The Environment

A rather alarming report stated that fourteen of the fifteen most polluted cities in the world are in India.[64] India's toxic air has been a cause of premature deaths to about 1,10,000 children in 2016, and India lost the highest number of children (60,987) under five years of age, in the world, due to exposure to outdoor air pollution.[65] This, coupled with India's aspiration to grow in double digits, with a focus on manufacturing, will be a challenge for the environment, and it is time that an institutional arrangement is made to address the issue in a planned manner.

A multi-pronged approach on awareness, action and sustainability is needed to address this major issue.

- The education system must incorporate field visits into the curriculum to sensitize children on what happens when the environment is neglected and narrate to them success stories of environmental preservation.
- Our country is blessed with abundant sunshine and the National Solar Mission, with its target of achieving an output of 100GW by 2022, should be aggressively pursued.
- Hydropower and nuclear power, both with relatively lower impact on the environment, must be leveraged for electricity generation. Also, considering the transformation of Japan in the '70s after setting up nuclear plants, we must give a thrust to nuclear energy for meeting the ever-increasing energy needs of the country
- All new buildings which are constructed should come with a mandate to have solar panels installed on them.

- All governing bodies of cities and towns should be tasked with coming up with a sustainable plan for generating power from solar energy.
- The use of coal as a means of power generation should be phased out.
- All vehicles across the country which are older than fifteen years should be scrapped.
- Only road tax and registration charges should be levied on electric vehicles, and they should be exempt from all other taxes.

Guaranteed Basic Amenities and Time-Bound Delivery of Services

Considering that the World Bank classifies India as a lower-middle-income country, taxes in India are very high.[66] Almost the entire population pays taxes, if one is to take into account direct and indirect taxes. However, every citizen must be assured of certain services and amenities in lieu of the taxes paid. If more than 40 per cent of the income of a middle-class family is to be paid as taxes, it is only fair that people should expect a return on their investment from the country. This return can take many forms: among others, good roads, uninterrupted supply of electricity, clean water, civic amenities, assured security, and prompt and efficient service from government offices. Therefore it is imperative that the government comes up with an institutional mechanism, coordinated at the highest levels, to ensure that citizens are not left wanting. One way to do this is to institute a Right to Time-Bound Delivery of Services Act, along the lines of the Right to Information Act, to ensure that response time on important issues and processes is time bound.

Taxes levied at tolls on highways must be phased out. The government collects road tax from vehicle owners and the high income tax we pay should, in any case, provide good roads. What we see is the opposite: even after paying road tax and toll levies, the quality of roads is pathetic in most parts of the country. From the metros to smaller cities and towns, roads are either potholed or constantly being dug up for some reason or the other. These are dangerous, and cause injuries and even deaths every year. There is no accountability in such cases, and must be fixed. The superintending engineer and public representative from the municipal ward must be taken to task, and mechanisms must be instituted through which damages can be recovered from them, along with the contractors. This same approach is required in all other areas in which citizens, even though they pay their taxes on time, or bring discrepancies and problems to the notice of local authorities but receive no redressal.

All certificates issued by the government must be digital and available online, and all land and other records must be digitized within five years. A system should be developed so that people don't have to visit a government office for work. This could be started in a phased manner and extended for every service and to every citizen in less than a decade.

Every department of the government should have a dashboard that displays the number of lives it impacts, the beneficiaries of its various schemes and functions, and the utilization rate for its services. We must move from stress on 'coverage' to 'usage' in all schemes rolled out by the government, and an impact assessment should be conducted for every scheme.

It is now time, also, to institute a rating system that applies to all government offices, to be used by the citizens who avail of their services. If the ratings fall below a certain level, the seniormost official of the office must be transferred and the official's increments stopped. If the below-par performance persists for three consecutive quarters, the official must be relieved from service.

National Defence and Homeland Security

The matters of national defence and homeland security are not just about safeguarding the nation and its citizens, but also carry within them the seeds of the country's pride and self-esteem. For instance I, for one, see no reason why we need permission from the US to buy oil from Iran or to buy weapons from Russia. As a sovereign nation, we must only recognize and honour sanctions if they are applied by the United Nations. And if we feel that even these sanctions imposed by the United Nations are unjust, or serve vested interests, we must abstain.

A Tough Stand on Terrorism: India has suffered and continues to suffer from terror across the border. Pakistan must be declared a 'Terrorist Nation' by India, and it must move a resolution in the UN to this effect. India granted Most Favoured Nation (MFN) status to Pakistan under the World Trade Organization. Pakistan, at no time, has granted India MFN status and has no plans to do so.[67] India must withdraw MFN status immediately. Terror, talks and trade can never go together.

Defence Preparedness: India fought its last major war forty-seven years ago. A lot of things since then have changed, but our defence expenditure remains low and, in fact, it has decreased between 2014 to 2018 and is at the lowest level since the 1962 war with China. The Twenty-Ninth Committee on Estimates of the Sixteenth Lok Sabha found this current situation 'unacceptable': that 60 per cent of our defence needs are imported, that there is a 'critical' shortage of ten or fifteen kinds of ammunition, and that there is also a shortage of the night-vision equipment.[68]

The countries with which we have gone to war still remain largely hostile, but their alignments, over the years, have changed, and so has the nature and science of warfare. We must do a lot more for the defence of our country. Our preparedness is only good insofar as we are not called upon to prove it. This is not good for a nation that is aspiring to grow at double digits and with expansionist and pro-terrorism neighbours that harbour anti-India designs.

India should not only be self-sufficient in terms of defence needs, but also become a net exporter of high-tech, miniature and long-range precision weapons as well as specialized equipment and technical knowhow for cyber and space warfare. We must plan, invest and work towards achieving this goal in a decade.

The other major lacuna, besides our shortcomings in defence equipment, is our lack of expertise in negotiating agreements on defence purchases and technology transfer as well as the logistics of supply and services. The armed forces lack this expertise and international suppliers have been able to take advantage of the loopholes to maximize their profits. So, this important issue must be addressed by the government urgently.

Foreign and Home Policy: Parallel to weapons procurement and development, India needs to recalibrate its foreign policy and come up with a bold plan for homeland security which calls for an integrated and live intelligence network driven by technology. Today, India is surrounded by neighbours who are influenced by expansionist powers who are doling out investments, this is dangerous and must be effectively addressed at the earliest. So, on the one hand, we have to address issues arising out of failing globalization and, on the other, rising 'Chinazation' (China expanding its footprint across nations under the veil of investments, infrastructure or aid).

Unfortunately, the details of what strategy India should adopt are beyond the scope of this present book, but let us not forget the unprovoked wars India has faced in the past, and their consequences. Today, more than direct and open wars, covert operations and cold wars cause irreparable damage. India needs to integrate its foreign, trade and defence policies to stay calm, focussed and secure. There has to be a high level of alertness, intelligence and pre-emptive action, 24X7, on all fronts. Most importantly, India needs to strengthen its own backyard in terms of ensuring food security and healthcare security, building a national logistics network, laying the groundwork for energy security (nuclear power is a must have), and bolstering the buying and spending capacity of its population.

A Seat at the High Table: India should reconsider its stand, and claim for itself a permanent seat at the United Nations Security Council (UNSC). If the UNSC does not have the world's largest democracy as its permanent member, it is not the forum India should aspire to be a part of. In fact, it is time that India takes a call on which multi-lateral bodies India should join and which it must exit. We cannot be taken for granted, despite being the largest democracy in the world. We must have a seat on the table of major multi-lateral agencies and with respectful voting rights, or a veto, as we have 1/6th of the population of the globe and we are the fastest growing economy, a peaceful nation and a vibrant democracy. We have a responsibility towards the progress and prosperity of the globe, and if we have no seat on the important multi-lateral bodies, India need not pay millions of dollars as annual payments to these multi-lateral agencies for membership. Also, we must be more active on promoting south-south collaboration.

Internal Acts of War: India will have to draft its policy on how it will deal with anti-state actors. In the absence of a clear and coherent policy, decision makers are sometimes at a loss to rise up to challenges; precious time is lost and this also occasionally leads to knee-jerk reactions that are not necessarily in the national interest. Also, once policies are made clear, anti-state actors will know the government's intent and this could function as a deterrent. In my view, acts of violence against the government and security forces should be treated as an act of war and responded to accordingly. Peaceful means should beget peaceful responses and arms and violence should have no place in negotiations. There should also be a national policy on illegal immigrants which should be implemented without ifs and buts.

Law Enforcement

Weak law enforcement has a direct impact on the nation and on society. This gives freedom to people to use the weakness as a shield and get away with impunity. It is time that effective steps are taken for implementing reforms in the judiciary, police policy and consumer rights, so that cases are speedily resolved and in a time-bound manner. Also, the procedures and policies of the government must be unambiguous, clear and simple, so that cases of frivolous litigation, and the discretion on the part of officials to take a decision, are reduced and remedial measures or outcomes are clear to citizens should something go wrong.

Here I will lay special focus on the legal processes to start a business. Why should we need multiple licenses from different departments? What purpose do these multiple licenses and approvals serve except contributing to delays, corruption and frustration for citizens? If a procedure doesn't contribute to making life simpler, it should be scrapped. All we should need before starting an enterprise is an online self-declaration of the entrepreneur, the details of the business, the investments made, and the nature of the goods and services dealt with. There should be no need to visit an office for any approvals or licenses. The office in charge of these matters should be empowered to conduct a spot check of the business, but with clearly defined dos and don'ts on what the inspection officials can and cannot do. There should be zero tax on the business in the first five years of its operation. There are two areas where clearly set out guidelines will be useful: in franchises, where clear laws are required to protect both the franchisee and the franchisor, and in the matter of businesses run from home. In the latter case, the system neither recognizes them, nor does it support them with clarity—except for lawyers, chartered accountants and doctors. This is unfortunate, because businesses run from home can become a major income source and a job creator and will make a huge difference to women entrepreneurs.

On the obverse, the government must also demand transparency from business owners. All false declarations or non-disclosures should lead to exemplary fines that will act as deterrents. Habitual defaulters should be black-listed and only allowed to start a business again after going through a paid training and induction programme at DEFA.

When signing work contracts, even if they are worth more than Rs 50,000, the signing parties should be able to register the contract by paying an online fee. Should there be a deficiency or default in the contract, the aggrieved party should be able to walk into a police station for the enforcement of their contracts. There is no reason why every small contract should become a matter for the courts. The majority of these cases amount to cheating; the police can easily verify the terms of the contract and enforce it. Else, there could be special courts dedicated to deal with such cases so that the cases are disposed of in less than a year. Also, the courts should impose a fine that acts as a deterrent for offenders and generates enough finance to run the enforcement system. This will ensure that the consumers are not taken for granted and courts are not saddled with cases.

Most importantly, the basic knowledge of rules and rights should be taught in school so that people are not mislead by law enforcers and undue harassment can be checked.

Agriculture and Rural Development

An ideal vision of rural India, and the future of profitable agriculture should, in my view, include the following: an educated young man, in jeans and T-shirt, driving a tractor and happily tilling his farmland; a middle-aged farmer running a guesthouse for tourists and visitors with all the modern amenities; and his wife and daughter running an enterprise in the guesthouse selling locally sourced handicrafts and organic produce.

Farmers and farming and rural development are two sides of the same coin. Fifty-nine per cent of our population is dependent, in some way or the other, on agriculture and 23 per cent of the GDP comes from it.[69] Thirteen per cent of the total exports of India, too, comes from agriculture.[70] Given the huge contribution of agriculture to the economy, and that jobs in other sectors are under threat due to automation and other technological advancements, it will be next to impossible to move the sheer number of people engaged in agriculture into other jobs. According to the Agricultural Census of India, 2011, an estimated 61.5 per cent of the

Indian population is rural and dependent on agriculture. The number of farming households is 15.96 crore. Thus we must focus on agriculture, in increasing production and profitability, as it still supports a huge segment of our population. Also, let us not forget that farmers played an important role in the freedom struggle and, today, they are fighting a struggle for their existence! We owe our cultivators a debt, payment for which is long overdue.

The present situation in this sector is not encouraging. As much as 67 percent of India's farmland is held by marginal farmers with holdings below one hectare, against the less than 1 per cent large holdings of 10 hectares and above. The average size per holding has been estimated as 1.15 hectare, which has shown a steady declining trend over various Agriculture Censuses since 1970–71.

In 2018, the National Bank for Agriculture and Rural Development released the NABARD All India Financial Inclusion Survey. The report painted a grim picture of agricultural indebtedness.[71]

- One out of two households save and the average savings is Rs 9,104
- One out of ten households invest and the average investment is Rs 62,734
- One in two households are indebted and and the average outstanding debt is Rs 91,407
- One out of four households are covered by insurance
- One in five households have pension cover

A comparison across two time periods, 2004–05 and 2011–12, also indicates that while there was an increase in the size of the total workforce in the country, the size of the agricultural workforce reduced by 3.05 crore people. The share of the agricultural workforce in the total workforce also declined from 56.7 per cent to 48.8 per cent in the same period.

Another cause for concern is that in 2010–11, the proportion of the net irrigated area to the net area sown was 45.70 per cent, which implies that irrigation is yet to reach as much as half the area under cultivation in India, and farmers rely entirely on the rains.

Our efforts at relieving the situation, too, have been far from satisfactory. We have witnessed the trend of farm-loan waivers, especially on the eve or soon after elections. These waivers are an attractive electoral proposition but do not provide long-term solutions to ensure the security, productivity, profitability and attractiveness of the farming profession. Further, waivers will have a direct impact on the country's rural development and the 'consumption index' or 'buying power' of India. Even increasing the minimum support price (MSP) for certain crops does not help in the short or the medium term, and might even backfire, as farmers will have to produce the crops first, and then the government will have to ensure adequate storage, transport and prompt payment for the purchases made on MSP. So, while these announcements are eye-catching, they are, at best, ad hoc arrangements and not a permanent solution to problems resulting from the long-standing systemic shortfalls faced by the farming community. We need a clear policy on loan waivers, nationally applicable, which spells out the conditions under which a loan or its interest can be deferred or and waived, and how the government expects to make up for the waivers.

We must also be careful of the corporatization of farming. America presents a cautionary example. In the 20th century, 3 crore Americans were engaged in agriculture; in the 21st century, increased mechanization, and corporatization, meant that 89 per cent of the agricultural production is done by a mere 3 lakh people. If we follow this same system, farmers, and rural India, will not only become poorer but it will create an infrastructural, economic and social burden on urban India which it cannot handle.

We must not close our eyes to the fact that food security is key to the economic and social security of the country. Hence, all issues impacting agriculture must be speedily addressed, always keeping in mind the wider issues.

Organic Farming or Genetically Modified (GM) Crops: India is sitting on a massive opportunity should we decide to produce organic and non-GM crops. This is the way forward in our quest to become the most valuable agricultural nation. The world over, people are moving towards organic produce and India must avoid getting influenced by corporate lobbies in the matter of GM crops.

Villages as Self-sustainable and Self-sufficient Economic Units: The Socio-Economic and Caste Census of 2011 revealed that out of 24.49 crore households, combining urban and rural areas, 17.97 crore stay in rural areas.[72] According to a report compiled by the National Sample Survey Office, 36 per cent of farmers are landless; the average monthly income of farmers in 2012–13 was Rs 6,426; about 52–56 per cent of households practising agriculture are debt-ridden; and farmers get only 20–30 per cent of the retail prices of their produce.[73] What we need, perhaps, is a situation where the government grants land to every landless farmer and where it creates and implements policies which ensure that 25 per cent of the total GDP growth comes from agriculture.

Increasing Productivity and Profitability: In India, the average yield of grains per hectare is 3.62 tonne, whereas in China it is 6.74 tonne, Vietnam produces 5.75 tonne per hectare.

The average yield of wheat is 3.03 tonne per hectare in India, whereas in France, it is 7.36 tonne per hectare and, in China, it is 5.04 tonne per hectare. In India, corn yield is 2.75 tonne per hectare whereas in the US it is 10.73 tonne; Argentina produces 6.6 tonne per hectare. The yield per hectare for pulses in India is 0.654 tonne per hectare; Canada produces 2.03 tonne per hectare and, China, 1.55 tonne.[74] Despite matchless biodiversity—India has forty-six of the sixty-four kinds of soils in the world and the total length of 445 rivers is two lakh kilometres—India still has a long way to go to focus on productivity and profits in agriculture in a planned manner.

Students taking up agriculture as a subject number only 0.65 per cent of the total, and agriculture education and research both need quantum leaps forward.

Subsidies in agriculture have increased to Rs 73,000 crores in the 2015–16 budget and, in addition, the subsidy on agriculture loans is also about 15,000 crores.[75] While these vast amounts are, of course, needed, we must also invest in rainwater conservation and irrigation, as half of the arable land in India does not have irrigation facilities.[76]

The decline of agriculture in Punjab should be upheld as a learning lesson. Punjab, which was once known for the Green Revolution, with a major portion of its population dependent on agriculture, is witnessing a decline in agriculture's contribution to the GDP. From a high of 32.67 per cent in 2004–05, it had fallen to 21.83 per cent in 2012–13.[77] Policymakers must take steps to ensure that what happened in Punjab is not repeated elsewhere in any other state.

Even if we take the above data as indicative, a few facts remain clear:

- A large portion of the population is dependent on agriculture

- The majority of farm holdings are small—below 1 hectare—and the average farm size is 1.5 hectare
- Less than half of all the farmlands in India have access to irrigation and depend on rains
- Farmers, and farmlands, are not connected to food-processing units and other opportunities to add value
- There is a huge impact of labour shortage in the farming sector, especially in the production of some major crops across various states.
- According to analyses by reputed organizations, like the NSSO in India and KPMG internationally, there has been a shift of the workforce from agriculture to the following non-agricultural sectors:
    - Primary sectors: Fisheries and forestry
    - Secondary sectors: Mining, manufacturing, construction, electricity, gas, steam and air conditioning supply, water supply, sewerage—waste management and remediation activities
    - Tertiary sectors: Wholesale and retail trade, motor vehicle and motorcycle repair, transportation and storage, financial and insurance activities.

These data, and facts, make the agenda for the government absolutely clear cut:

- All government strategies have to be crop specific and region specific
- The migration of labour and the consequent shortage has to be urgently addressed
- The irrigation of agricultural land has to be pursued in mission mode. The first step is to create an action plan in which there is a clear segregation of arable and dry land; irrigated, non-irrigated and rainfed areas,

and a roadmap which will ensure the provision of irrigation facilities to non-rainfed areas

- Support the move from chemical fertilizers to herbicides
- Implement crop-insurance schemes at subsidized rates or free of cost
- The Rythu Bandhu scheme in Telangana is a good example to look at in terms of supporting farmers. Also, Odisha is giving an assistance of Rs 10,000 under the KALIA (Krushak Assistance for Livelihood and Income Augmentation), which aims to cover 0.74 crore households, including the landless. So just an increase in the MSP as a standalone step will not solve farm distress. The scheme should start before the crop is sown, and only then will the farmer be in a better position to reap the harvest and claim the benefits of MSP
- Support farmers by providing them high-end mechanization, implements and other tools they need. In fact, a good plan is to institute farmers' cooperatives in every district which will buy these equipment, and maintain and lease them to farmers to reduce the cost of inputs. This will also provide a boost to the manufacturing industries associated with agriculture
- Research should be intensified on increasing productivity and sustainability in agriculture
- Farmers should be trained and equipped with the necessary tools to manage the entire chain of production, from farm to fork, and this is the only step which will retain people in agriculture and make it worthwhile for them. This also calls for the government to invest in a major way in cold storage,

processing, road and rail connectivity to the nearest towns and even going online. Given that 7–13 per cent (numbers vary from source to source) of exports is from agriculture, we need to enhance agricultural exports from the current 13 percent to 25 percent to boost rural India through agriculture

- Crops such as millets which have a major presence in the health-food segment should be given focus and government should create an institutional setup for the export of such crops and to promote them internationally. Agricultural produce that is unmistakably Indian, such as Basmati, should be made part of an extensive branding exercise which will make it a multi-crore industry for farmers.
- Organic farming should be given major institutional support, perhaps through an organization such as the Organic Farming Corporation of India. Also, India must, as a policy, take a call on whether it wishes to become dependent on chemical fertilizers or move to organic agriculture. The world is moving towards organic and other natural consumption trends, it might be a good idea to follow suit. This will be tough, and mean resisting pressure from the fertilizer lobby, the chemical industry, and producers of GM crops, but will be in the best and long-term interest of farmers and national security.
- GM crops should be banned in India for farming and for sale, and there should be a special labelling (Black dot with GM written) on products that have genetically modified ingredients in it.
- MSME enterprises must be linked to agriculture.
- Farmers need government support in marketing their produce.

- We must aim to triple our exports in the agricultural sector in the next decade.

Above all, the overarching goal of all these policies and ideas is to get the youth to move towards agriculture, start the reverse migration of citizens from metros to rural areas. These twin targets are our ultimate tests, and will constitute our goal of 'Happy Farmer—Wealthy India!'

Rural India—Villages as Economic Units

About two-thirds of India lives in villages. But the fact is that, despite Panchayati Raj, and other schemes which the Centre and the states have implemented over the decades, the basic infrastructure for the majority of Indians who live in villages does not exist. Therefore, the overarching target for the government of the day is to bridge the divide between the so-called 'Bharat' and 'India', and aim at providing uniform access to the same basic infrastructure to all Indians. In fact, given the clean environment and open spaces in rural India, we should aim to build such an infrastructure of connectivity, health and education there that reverse migration should start by 2025. Else we will have failed the majority of the country's population. I still recall this oft-repeated political slogan from Maharashtra: 'Make Mumbai like Shanghai'. But that did not happen. What we need to try is to make smaller towns 'mini Mumbai' or 'mini Chandigarh'. Rather than trying to ape the size and scale of large metro cities, it might be a better idea to identify focus towns in each state and invest in their development. Big towns should henceforth receive funds only for maintenance or become self-sufficient in generating their own resources over the next decade.

Villages need to have a sustainable model for economy, infrastructure and environment, and this model should not just be sustainable and self-sufficient, but also attractive for the urban population to start moving towards the countryside. The town nearest to any village should be not more than a 40-minute drive. We should be able to come up with a model which eliminates the difference between rural and urban areas on the basis of infrastructure. We need 'smart and self-sufficient village clusters', as all villages do not have a population that is adequate for making them self-sustainable. Village-level self-sufficiency means that value addition, linked to agriculture produce, should happen in villages and not just in urban areas. If we focus only on building food-processing units in bigger towns, the urban–rural divide will only grow further and not lessen. We need a plan to build world-class SMEs in processing food and agriculture produce, handicrafts etcetra, and link them to the nation through online sales platforms so that retailers and consumers can be supplied directly. Hence we need sufficient packaging units in rural India with logistic facilities, including road connectivity, so that farmers are able to make the best use of modern development to achieve higher profit. Also, besides economic avenues for rural India, we need to make life more vibrant, and for that to happen, we need to ensure proper avenues for sports, culture and arts, and entertainment as well. The success of all these steps will result in more and more people turning to agriculture and moving to the countryside because of the quality of life and increased earning capacity.

Therefore, the ministries of agriculture, rural development, transport and MSME must work hand-in-hand to uplift the Indian economy in totality. There has to be an overarching vision of these ministries for rural upliftment and integration. Working in silos will never deliver results, even if investments are ramped up.

District-Level Self-Sufficiency

One of the major challenges for a large and diverse country like India is that a few large metro cities such as Mumbai, Pune, Gurugram, Delhi and Bengaluru, have become attractive destinations for people seeking to migrate. However, it is precisely because of this demand that their population and infrastructure is under constant pressure. This shows that the rest of the country has not caught up with the changing needs of the times and the residents of these 'left behind' towns are migrating to the so-called bigger or better towns and cities to take advantage of the opportunities available. Now, with the plan to set up 100 smart cities, this divide is going to become further complicated! In addition to the existing urban-rural-tribal divide, we will also factor in the division between the SMART city and the non-SMART city. The goal for the country's policy makers should be to ensure that, for all purposes, district-level self-sufficiency should be the goal for setting up 'development infrastructure'. Which implies that civil supplies, healthcare, education and training, and jobs, should be available at the district level. The district administration should be managing affairs in such a manner that local residents should be an asset to the administration, and the taxes (and other financial resources) collected should be sufficient (if not surplus), to provide the best of services to the districts. Of course, the state administration and the Centre should handhold and provide support to some districts which have remained backwards but, for the major part, the district administration under the mayor (the city CEO) should be held responsible for the development and delivery of services to its population. This calls for a new approach to develop infrastructure, local industry, trade, professionals and entrepreneurs to cater to the needs of the district economy. Every district should come up with a vision document of what it needs to do and achieve in the next fifteen, ten and five years, based on a yearly plan, goals and deliverables. If we fail to achieve this, India's development will only increase disparities and the resultant patterns of migration will create a disproportionate burden on infrastructure.

Small Traders and Retail Stores

With 1.4 crore (numbers vary as per estimates) retailers across the length and breadth of India, the country's consumer and employment markets are, in a way, dependent on this trade channel. The worst decision of successive governments has been to open the retail and wholesale market to Foreign Direct Investment (FDI). Large-scale retailers are unwelcome even in the largest, most developed economies, and most locals have problems with them for their role in squeezing profit margins and taking away jobs. In 2013, on a visit to Michigan in the US, I saw a large number of signboards lining the sides of major roads proclaiming: 'Back off Wal-Mart. Not our towns!!'

We must consider this reality. The collective profit earned off the consumption behaviour of a combined population of 130 crore people could be drained out of India if multinational retailers capture total market share, a reality that is imminent in the next few years. This will wipe out small mom-and-pop stores, small-scale traders, and create massive unemployment. Large-scale retailers operate on a profit-per-employee model and, with increased automation, even more shedding of jobs and the accumulation of profits and revenues in the hands of few corporations is likely. For a large lower middle-class country like India, the answer lies in creating a distributed growth model, with MSMEs as the highest priority of the government. So this is what we must expect of the government:

- Withdraw FDI in retail (even online retail), or limit it to no more than 25 per cent
- Seventy per cent of goods and products have to be sourced locally in India. Imports should only be allowed for products that cannot be produced in India. Overdependence on imports will dilute the 'Make in India' programme and even render it ineffective
- Provide institutional support, with hard and soft infrastructure, and in a planned manner, to small-scale traders and retailers so that they can easily upgrade and remain competitive. Set up the DEFA and task it to give recommendations to retail establishments in any given area or city
- Even the existing domestic online retail space should have offline fulfilment centres, through existing retailers, so that employment in retail, and the segment itself, can grow. Innovation is totally missing in this segment, and we need to ensure innovation,

across the value chain, to enhance profits and retain jobs

- Also, the rights and interests of consumers must be defined and protected. Retailers (whether small or large) take consumers for granted as it is a pain to take up issues to consumer courts. The government machinery must ensure that the grievance redressal system is credible, just and efficient so that any matter does not linger in the courts for years. Consumer rights should also be protected against cartelization and other actions that are detrimental to consumers.

Marginalized Communities Need a Giant Leap

Marginalized communities refer to individuals or groups who are away from mainstream society—women, children, Scheduled Castes, Scheduled Tribes, persons with disabilities, migrants, and others.[78] Despite the efforts of successive governments, marginalized communities have not come at par with the other strata of society, and neither have they integrated with the mainstream. It is clear that support from multiple schemes over the decades is not working in the real sense. There is a need for us to innovate on this issue, with mission mode projects, all with predefined sunset clauses that set deadlines, and with clearly defined deliverables. Moreover, we must demand identifiable results in a time-bound manner. While many communities, especially among the Scheduled Tribes, need support and upliftment, a wholesale approach is not possible, and care must be taken to preserve their indigenous knowledge, wealth and culture and, at the same time, we have to ensure that they also remain connected to the developments witnessed by other sections of the society.

These are some key areas in this sector which need focus:

- We need a systematic approach to support children from marginalized families from birth so that they can come up to par with those who have had the advantages of privilege since birth. Plans are required to ensure good health, sound education, productive vocational training, fruitful travel and successful entrepreneurship. The upliftment of girls requires especial focus. All of these advantages should be made available to these children near their place of residence so that migration becomes unnecessary.
- Financial incentives for good performance in school and in keeping good health will help boost morale and performance, and encourage people to be at par with the best.
- It is an injustice to the poor if reservations provided by the government are not extended to financially weaker sections of society.
- We need public libraries, institutional support for self-help groups, and special entrepreneurship schemes for the marginalized. The effects of these will be dramatic, especially when role models are created who can inspire everyone else.
- Population stabilization and control has an important role to play in the long-term prosperity and upliftment of all Indians. These must be taken up on a high priority basis to ensure that population growth matches the resources needed, the replacement ratio is balanced, and demographic imbalance is avoided.

Women's Safety and Gender Equality

The best way to evaluate a secure and a safe society is to examine one vital parameter: the safety and freedom of women. This parameter is also a measure of the country's cultural and social standards, its law and order situation, and the judicial system of the nation.

Cases of violence against women are on the rise. The perpetrators of these crimes come from all strata of society. That this should be so indicates the scale of the challenge we must address. This is a complex issue but a few salient points are inescapable:

- There is a complete disconnect of the young from ancient values and culture; a problem that originates from a flawed education system.
- Unrestricted exposure to media and the internet. The bombardment of information of all kinds, with no time for assimilation or reflection, has transformed the age-old value systems and culture of Indian society.
- Poor law enforcement also plays a big role. Today, cases aren't solved even in a lifetime, and if solved, the system of justice delivery is extremely slow.

The issue of ensuring women's safety calls for a multi-sectoral approach and a combination of steps—right from a complete overhaul of the systems of education, law enforcement and the judiciary. Above all, it is up to us to find sound, current role models for our children today. We cannot keep going back to history, to previous centuries, to find role models for the modern age. We will have to create a system, and this is an important step and a subset of the lengthier and much broader process of development. This needs to start in a carefully planned manner and the government has a key role to formulate a multi-sectoral approach, else Indian society, known for its wisdom and values since ancient times, will wither away faster than we can imagine.

Senior Citizens

According to the Sample Registration System (SRS) 2013 of the Census of India, the population of senior citizens was 12.10 crores, growing at 3 per cent a year.[79] By that reckoning, the population of the elderly in India is 13 crores and, by 2025, the number of senior citizens will be 15.8 crores and account for 11 per cent of the population. According to the Senior Care Industry Report compiled by the Confederation of Indian Industry (CII), the number of senior citizens living in rural areas—7.7 crores—is almost double the number living in urban areas—3.9 crores.[80] As a country, we are already in the category of an 'ageing nation'. Also, we should not forget that India is also a lower and middle-income (LMIC) country, as classified by the World Bank.[81] If we add the former category to the latter, we will become a LMIAC (lower and middle-income and ageing country). This is a fair assessment of the challenge we face in the future.

We need to evaluate the needs for our senior citizens with the target year of 2050 in mind. If we have not, we are heading for a major crisis. The lack of a plan for senior citizens will alter our demographic dividends due to the dependency ratio. By 2050, the number of senior citizens living in India (30 crores) which will be almost equivalent to the size of the population of the US in 2018 (32.8 crores).[82] With a declining fertility rate and the increased life expectancy of our general population, we face a serious challenge from old age dependency ratio (the ratio of older dependents to the working age population between 15–64 years) heading towards us.

We must work on specifics in terms of the actual requirements for this population and given the transition of society to the nuclear family system, make our plans in advance. We must take into consideration multiple steps, with long-term planning, which, among others, should include the following:

- We must make provisions for the social security and safety of senior citizens.
- Create incentives which will boost the domestic savings rate for pensions and the post-retirement expenditure of senior citizens.
- We need innovation in the nature of financial products and offerings made available to senior citizens so that they become financially independent.
- The health of senior citizens should be a high priority and gerontology as a field of specialization needs to be attended to on a priority basis. We must create a specialized cadre of health professionals which will cater to the needs of this huge population segment.
- We have to find ways to productively channelize the experience and expertise which they have gathered over the years even after they are retired. If people are fit and willing to contribute to society post retirement, they will be a matchless asset to the nation and to society. We need a special skills development programme for senior citizens.
- Guidelines and laws are needed to ensure that children take care of their parents.
- It is with the move from the agrarian to the service economy that Indian society has shifted towards a culture of nuclear families. Now that this culture is prevalent, we will need a nationwide network of communities and residential complexes specially designed for senior citizens, we also need old age homes and hospices as well as especially skilled people to take care of senior citizens.

- We need clear guidelines which will govern the setting up and running of these homes and hospices.
- We should also not forget that senior citizens offer great business and service opportunities. The service opportunities have been outlined above. In terms of business, there is a need for a) a savings rate of about 30 per cent; b) a planned pension scheme; and c) a health savings account in which young people make investments that will take care of their increasing healthcare needs in old age. These three carry great potential for financial companies to create a sound source of revenue.

Social Security

Social security will ensure the attractiveness of the Indian market and the sustainability of the economy in the long run, when the dependency ratio becomes skewed. It is also a key feature of a government that cares.

The picture that is generally given out by the government, and amplified by the media, is that only about 3–4 per cent of the total number of citizens earning a taxable income actually pay taxes and, therefore, its resources are limited. This is a terribly wrong picture and quite far from reality. In fact, a tax—various sales taxes earlier and, now, the single Goods and Services Tax (GST)—is levied on almost all the products sold in the country. Therefore each citizen, whether a well-to-do person or someone living below the poverty line, pays taxes on consumer products and services. Also, some middle-income people like us pay a 'triple tax'—an income tax, corporate taxes and, finally, taxes levied on products and services. Every Indian pays tax one way or the other. Hence the government of the day must ensure that when it takes away a percentage of every single rupee I earn, it assures me of some level of service in lieu. We will be well within our rights to demand social security due to disability, or post retirement.

To start with, the government can invest in setting up an adequate number of homes and hospices, of good standard, for senior citizens and the differently abled so that citizens who are unable to take care of themselves, whether due to advanced age or a chronic physical problem, have support from some social system that is funded and managed by the government. The government must look after the population that does its duty by paying taxes. There is no justification, otherwise, for such a high rate of tax.

The government has also failed to deliver on the quality of life even though it levies high taxes. It is the duty of the government to provide clean drinking water, yet people in most cities and villages must make their own arrangements to find potable water. Why has the government left education and health to the private sector, which does not let go of any opportunity to extort money from the common man? And, in cases of extortion, there is no grievance redressal mechanism either. In the field of healthcare, what can be a worse indictment than government officials and ministers travelling to the UK, US or Europe if they fall sick? Don't they have confidence in the Indian healthcare system? And are these visits abroad available to the common man? We must build a quality-driven, and accountable healthcare system that delivers the best possible care.

The Economy—Moving Towards a Distributed Growth Model

National aspirations and political compulsions must be balanced; any imbalance will compromise India's present and the future. We must move towards a distributed-growth model as a pre-requisite for ensuring sustainable growth and creating a recession-proof economy. The current economic model of India is unsustainable. This is a model where the accumulation of growth happens at the hands of a few people (big investors and industrialists). Such growth will lead naturally to disparities between the rich and the poor. A few datasets illustrate these disparities:

- In 2018, 73 per cent of the wealth generated went to the richest 1 per cent, while 67 crore Indians, who comprise the poorest half of the population, saw only a 1 per cent increase in their wealth.[83]
- The average Indian individual has net assets of approximately USD 6,600.[84]
- There are approximately 3,30,000 high net worth individuals (HNWIs) living in India, each with net assets of USD1 million or more.[85]
- There are approximately 20,700 multi-millionaires living in India, each with net assets of USD10 million or more.[86]
- There are 1,064 millionaires living in India, each with net assets of USD100 million or more.[87]
- There are 119 billionaires living in India, each with net assets of USD1 billion or more. India has a particularly large number of billionaires—only two other countries, the US and China, have more.[88]

According to an analysis made by the economists Sandhya Krishnan and Neeraj Hatekar, the following is the population-wise break-up for different economic classifications. The income threshold is in terms of spending per capita per day.[89]

Category	Income threshold	2004-05 (Population)	2011-12 (Population)
Poor	< $2	77.73 Crore	57.48 Crore
Lower-middle	$2-4	23.78 Crore	44.66 Crore
Middle –middle	$4-6	4.54 Crore	10.85 Crore
Upper-middle	$6-10	2.1 Crore	4.95 Crore
Affluent	>$10	75 lacs	2.29 Crore

A few relevant statistics. The total number of credit card holders, until August 2018, is 4,10,28,843[90] and the total number of live Kisan Credit Cards, until March 2018, is 4,56,88,100.[91]

The total number of credit card holders also includes people holding two or more cards. Therefore, the actual number of card holders is a maximum of 2 crore. If we add to this the total number of live Kisan Credit Cards issued until March 2018—4,56,88,100—the total number of card holders, including the Kisan Credit Cards, won't add up to more than 8.66 crore. And if we factor in the number of people holding multiple cards, the number could be lesser. We must also note that the credit limits on the KCCs are lower than others, and users are more likely to use them for making seasonal purchases and according to need. Therefore, if we assume that it is only the middle class and the rich who have credit cards, and if we combine the 'Affluent' and 'Upper-middle' categories, the number of Indians who have actual discretionary buying and spending power is a little above 7 crores—about 5.38 per cent of the total population.

Even if we add the holders of the KCCs—despite their lower buying and spending capacity—to this, the total number does not cross 12 crores. The conclusion is clear: less than 10 per cent of the total population is driving the economy and deriving benefits from its growth. Ten per cent of the citizenry cannot be expected to take care of 90 per cent of the population. Increased spending creates more opportunities to earn; all citizens need increased spending power and only a new economic model, the 'Distributed Growth Model' can deliver this.

Also, a look at the FDI inflow comparison gives us an interesting insight (see p. 123). The FDI inflows for 2016 and 2017 make it clear that India's population does not have the spending capacity to serve the investors' needs in terms of consumption.[92]

For 2016 and 2017, even much smaller developing countries like Brazil. Brazil has population of 210 million (21 crore) and is smaller than Uttar Pradesh in terms of population, which has a population of 227 million (22.7 crore) had about 50 per cent higher FDI inflow than India and Mexico (Mexico's population is about half that of Uttar Pradesh) still received about 75 per cent of the FDI inflow as compared to India. These numbers show that the economic proposition of India is not commensurate with its huge population base. It is pertinent to quote that the consumption-driven economy is the most predominant pattern which applies to economic growth across Asia, and the key to FDI in an economy.[93] If we compare 2017 and 2018, it only reinforces this point (see p. 124):[94]

In 2018, smaller economies like Spain, with a little over 4.6 crore people, received Rs 4,97,000 crores as FDI. Australia, whose population matches the annual growth of India's, got an FDI of Rs 4,40,200 crores and Brazil, with a

FDI Inflows, Top 20 Host Economies 2016 and 2017
(Billions of Dollars)

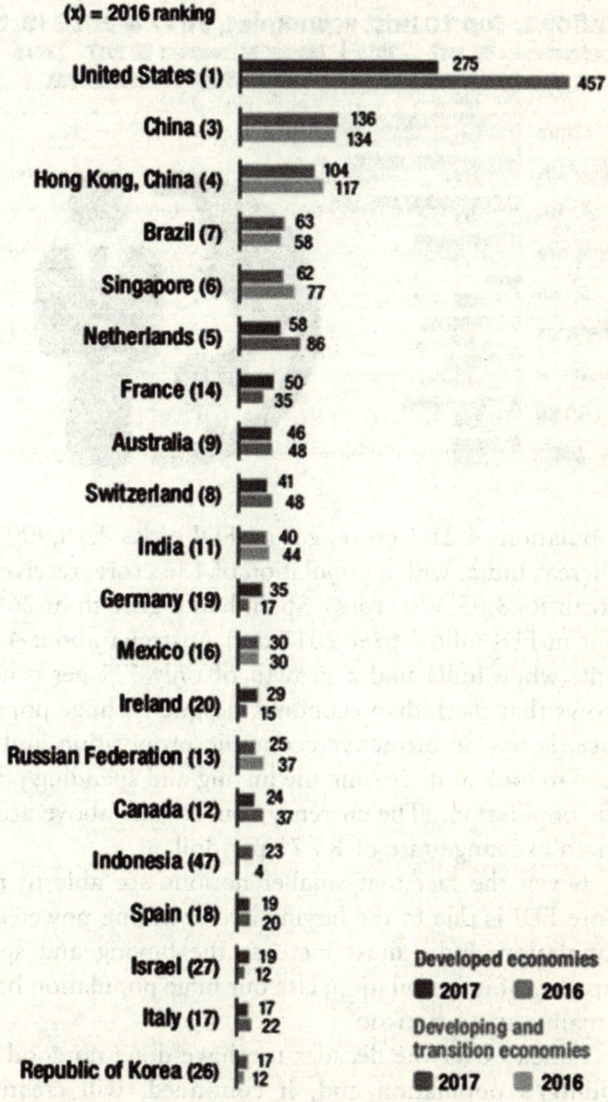

Source: UNCTAD, FDI/MNE database (www.unctad.org/fdistatistics).

population of 21.1 crore, got an FDI of Rs 4,18,900 Crore, whereas India, with a population of 136 crore, received FDIs worth Rs 3,05,300 crores. Spain had a growth of 268.4 per cent in FDI inflow over 2017 and Australia about 40.9 per cent, while India had a growth of only 7.5 per cent. This shows that the Indian economy, despite its huge population base, is not an attractive economic proposition and so we need to look at increasing the buying and spending power of our population. (The currency conversions above are based on an exchange rate of Rs 71 per dollar.)

Given the fact that smaller nations are able to rake in more FDI is due to the buying and spending power of their population. India must increase the buying and spending capacity of its population; else our huge population base will remain a mere statistic.

Policies over the decades too have done no good to this country's population and, if continued, will create more divide between haves and have-nots; they will increase the undue influence of the rich and create large-scale unrest due to wealth accumulated in the hands of a few.

The solution lies in fuelling the economy through MSMEs, cooperatives and Self-Help Groups (SHGs), and linking them to the population in the countryside engaged in agriculture. We need a special programme to uplift families that earn below Rs 10,000 a month. Also, we need to learn lessons from Germany, a strong and a resilient economy which remained relatively untouched by the recession of 2008. The key to that country's success is Mittelstand, a policy approach in which SMEs receive state patronage and support and they, in turn, make the biggest contribution to high employment and productivity. Here are some interesting statistics:[95]

- More than 99 per cent of all German firms (3.7 million) belong to the SME category.
- SMEs contribute almost 52 per cent of the total economic output of Germany, totalling a turnover of 2 trillion euros.
- SMEs employs 60 per cent of employees subject to social security contributions and take in 83.2 per cent of the total number of trainees hired.
- 95 per cent of Germany's SMEs are family-owned.
- German SMEs are the most innovative in Europe and supply goods all over the world. There are some 1,300 world market leaders among the SMEs which make up the Mittelstand.
- These market leaders are in a variety of sectors ranging from electrical, engineering and industrial products.
- The Mittelstand SMEs are a major contributor to a lower percentage of unemployed youth in Germany than in many other European nations.

- The website www.make-it-in-germany.com is a staunch supporter of the Mittelstand initiative.

How do we implement a successful, working replica of the Mittelstand model in India? To start with, we must have a clearsighted plan for MSMEs, cooperatives and self-help groups (SHGs), with keen focus on innovation even as we ensure that the products from these establishments meet the highest standards of quality. These enterprises are based in small towns across the country and they need to be supported, not just with finances, but with strategy and quality systems to ensure that their products and services are at par with the best in the world. Without a clear roadmap, training and stringent quality control, the replication of the Mittelstand model can quickly backfire. Entrepreneurs will take the loans made available to them, start their businesses and, in the absence of market knowledge and guidelines, fail, seek fresh loans, fail again and get into a vicious cycle of debt. Or their loans will become non-performing assets (NPAs) for the lenders, creating a bubble which could be much bigger than even farm loans. The solution to all these problems lies in setting up the DEFA.

District Employment and Entrepreneurship Facilitation Agency (DEFA)

Most small businesses fail due to lack of institutional support and an understanding of how the market operates, what the consumption trends are, what the needs of the buying population are and what their buying power is. These data are rarely available with officials siting in their air-conditioned chambers in state capitals or at the Centre, in Delhi. These officials never or rarely pay visit to the actual site of the business or interact with the beneficiaries. Even if they do, such interactions are stage managed for publicity. From the government's perspective, there is an important reason for the government to set up the DEFA. The government is a default stakeholder in any company, to the tune of 26 to 35 per cent. This is because the government takes taxes on the income of the companies and at present, the minimum corporate tax is 26 per cent including cess and maximum corporate tax is 34.95.[96] At the same time, the government has only the upside, with its profits in business, and no downside since it has no liability towards losses. Therefore, as a responsible stakeholder, the government has all the reasons to set up the DEFA, not just to ensure ease of doing business, but also be a facilitator for success of the business enterprise so that it continues to enjoy the income from its stake in the venture.

Most small businesses are set up with loans taken from moneylenders or banks, or with capital gained by selling property or valuables. Should the business fail, whether from a lack of knowledge of operating conditions, or other reasons, the entrepreneur and, in collateral damage, his family will suffer.

To illustrate: On the Panvel–Matheran road in the outskirts of the Panvel area in Navi Mumbai, there is a stretch of 5 kilometres, in an area which is not even densely populated, where there are four 'supermarkets' and a fifth 'supermarket' is coming up. This, despite the presence of an umpteen number of road-side grocers. It is sure that the road-side grocers will eventually have to close down because of competition from these 'supermarkets' and, eventually, even these 'supermarkets' will have to shut down due to competition amongst themselves, or to some big-ticket retailer setting up shop in the area. These closures will hit the local economy hard and cause huge losses, not only to those who invested in the business but also those whom they employed.

This is where the DEFA could play a vital role. The DEFA should be set up by the Ministry of MSME in each district, with extension offices in the towns which comprise the district. This organization can be a partnership between the MSME ministry and local business schools, and other professionals who can be hired from time to time or as and when needed. The role of the DEFA should be two-fold—to provide guidance to MSMEs and, in the longer term, to boost the per capita GDP in the district through the following measures:

- Set the vision for the district under its jurisdiction.
- Conduct research on business opportunities and their viability. Conduct market analysis studies and project the needs of the local population, its consumption trends and consumer behaviour, and define the parameters for the viability of a particular business in an area or locality, based on the needs of the local population, and the potential for exports.
- Identify clusters in every district for production units and their needs in terms of machinery and manpower.
- Impart training for businesses that are based on local needs.
- Create internship and 'earn while you learn' programmes, and find appropriate opportunities for the professional engagement of senior citizens, based on their skills and fitness levels.
- Develop and implement quality assurance for products and services.
- Become a nodal point for the disbursement of government loans and grants, based on the viability of businesses.
- The permit system of starting a business, for example,

owning a cab, should be done away with, and the DEFA should be the entity which decides how many businesses can operate, based on its viability studies.

- Impart training and skill-development exercises to cater to local business needs.
- Identify and develop quality management systems and ensure their deployment.
- Business units and entrepreneurs should be registered under the 'One India, Single Window—One Business, One Registration' principle with the DEFA.
- Institute a district-level ranking of ease of doing business across the nation and institute a Liveability Index. All cities must be rated by its citizens on safety, access and connectivity, public amenities, taxes, health, education, environment, entertainment, employment, entrepreneurship and responsive administration and public representatives. This will lead to a healthy competition among cities to become more citizen and business friendly.

The DEFA can be made self-sustainable by charging a small fee for its syndicate reports and studies, and for conducting customized market research as assessment and business feasibility studies for an entrepreneur. For women entrepreneurs, it can discount its services by 50 per cent. DEFA is a must have for every town. It is needless to mention that for the 7,935 towns in India, it will increase the available employment by at least 100 times, and contribute to making many more successful entrepreneurs. The DEFA should look comprehensively at all sectors, including agriculture and small retail stores; it should also forecast the needs of all small- and middle-scale employees and workers such as barbers, cobblers, teachers, farmers, daily labourers, cooks, nannies and security guards, among others. Also, for all funds related to the entrepreneurship schemes of the state and the central government, the DEFA should be the nodal agency for disbursement, and this agency can charge 1 per cent of the fund as its service fee for disbursal and for providing viability reports, guidance and ongoing business consultancy.

The DEFA should serve as an aggregator for making group purchases on behalf of its entrepreneurs to provide them a platform for collective bargaining in the purchase of raw materials. This is where the smaller logistics firms under DEFA, aggregators in villages and small production factories in towns will create a 'distributed growth model' for India. Of all the government tenders for purchases and contracts, 60 per cent should be reserved for domestic bidders and 20 per cent for startups. The remaining 20 per cent can be sent out to global bidders, in the absence of which, orders may be awarded to domestic bidders.

It is hoped that this organization will change the entire landscape of the self-employed as well as that of professionals, the retail sector with its small-scale enterprises, and small-scale industry in the country. It will be the biggest contributor to establishing viable and profitable businesses and mass employment opportunities.

All this will not only make Indian economy resilient, but also provide employment and entrepreneurship opportunity, mapping facilities across the country. If this project is implemented successfully as envisioned, we can create an E-MAP—an Employment and Entrepreneurship MAP—for every Indian town and village in the next three years. We could easily identify the kind of workforce and training we need for India and address, to a large extent, the unemployment and failure rate in the country.

The other important exercise which the DEFA should also

undertake is the creation of a Vishwakarma App Programme (VKAP) for the workforce engaged as labourers in the building and construction industry which will address the issue of identity, productivity and security of about 5 crore individuals.

The Vishwakarma App Programme (VKAP)

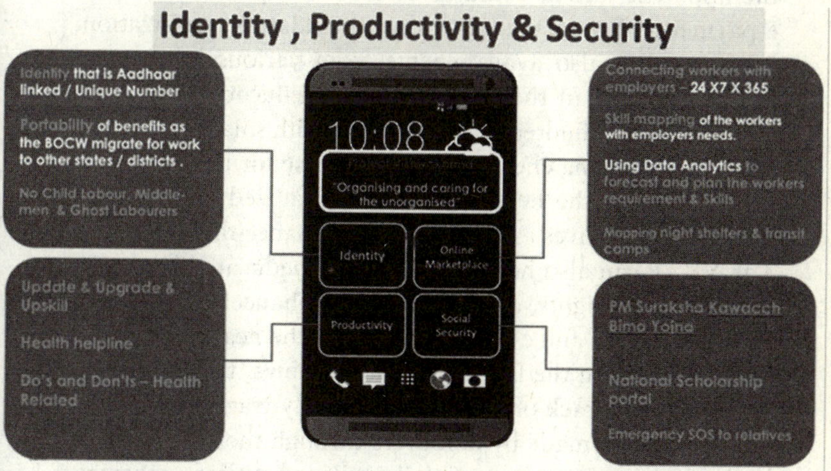

The labour force in the construction sector numbers upwards of 5 crore, but not only are they unorganized, they also face a lot of hardship when it comes to finding the right work or even getting their due share in terms of remuneration or benefits from government schemes. Manual labourers standing on roadsides in all weather conditions, waiting for someone to hire them, present a common sight. A lot of the time they may be standing in the wrong place, and keep standing there fruitlessly. And even though there may be a demand for their particular skill, the demand may be in another area.

The VKAP can list the workers available—with details of their skills and work experience, along with a verifiable unique id—across India as well as a list of all potential employers. Therefore, a manual labourer need not wait in Delhi when he or she can get suitable work in Noida. The VKAP can help map needs based on availability and potential employers can connect with prospective employees through the app. The VKAP could also serve as a platform for the e-payment of wages and, with a mandatory registration, labourers can also avail benefits from various schemes of the government in the areas of health, education, pension, scholarship for children and insurance. With smartphones and 4G data becoming cheaper, it makes sense for us to leverage technology for the benefit of the unorganized labour force and make their lives easier, as well as enhance their earnings. The VKAP can also help these mostly uneducated labourers to know their rights, aid in their skill enhancement through online tutorials, and even guide them to the nearest available night shelters. In the larger scheme of things, the VKAP can also help keep track of the number of daily-wage jobs created and the money made by labourers through them. These will be helpful in designing specially tailored welfare schemes, prevent cheating by employers and ensure appropriate wages, preferably through e-payment. We will also be to address the problem of ghost labour, which represent a huge drain on available resources, and ease the migration of labour. The VKAP can also be extended and applied to the informal sector in other areas like the hiring of household assistants and tourism-related employment.

Similarly, as mentioned earlier, we must also work towards creating an E-MAP (the Employment and Entrepreneur MAP), linked with the DEFA at the backend to enlist all the daily wage earners, self-help group members, BOCWs, entrepreneurs, and MSMEs on a national platform, which will ensure that people are able to search for gainful employment.

The DEFA, the VKAP and the E-MAP can become the biggest facilitators of the distributed growth model. They will ensure that the wealth generated through these businesses remains localized in small towns and villages and with the lower and middle-income class.

One fact is crystal clear—the value of the nation's currency not only mirrors the strength of its economy, it is directly proportional to it. In my opinion, there is a big difference between economic growth and economic development, and, currently, we are overly focussed on economic growth, as represented by the GDP. Economic development is a broader concept which includes GDP per capita, and other indicators like poverty alleviation, social justice, income distribution, political freedom, pollution, and equality of income. It reflects how income is spent, while economic growth only indicates a narrow concept of national income. The actions of successive governments are overly focussed on economic growth and if we are to adopt economic development in its broadest sense, I think it will be appropriate to rename the Ministry of Finance the Ministry of Economic Development.

To sum up: the current economic growth model of India is ad hoc and lopsided. Hence we need to define a clear path of transition into the new economic model, which should be about 'Distributed Growth'. This new model is based on us achieving multiple targets: ensuring the self-sufficiency of districts; creating wealth and distributing it amongst the lower and middle classes rather than a few big business houses and MNCs; a drastic increase in public goods—in education, health and infrastructure; ensuring the availability of capital; removing bureaucratic legacies and red tape; and, most importantly, reducing taxes—the government must understand that reducing taxes puts more money in the hands of citizens which, consequently, will increase their buying power and boost revenue. The DEFA, the VKAP and the E-MAP will be important tools for us to achieve these overarching plans.

Making a Choice between Fiscal Deficit and Investment Deficit

Currently, global rating agencies, bookish economists and governments are really concerned about a goal that goes against the interest of an LMIC—maintaining a fiscal deficit of not more than 3.3 per cent. (Fiscal deficit is what occurs when the government's expenditure exceeds the revenue it generates. This revenue does not include the money which the government has borrowed.)

Also, if we consider where the government spends its rupee, it seems difficult for any government to garner funds needed to invest into massive capex needs for infrastructure and job creation.[97] India will remain a capital hungry nation for the next two decades if it has to break into the league of developed nations. Given that for every rupee spent by the government, 27 paise goes into subsidies and interest payments (9 paise on subsidies and 18 paise on interest payments), can it indulge in electoral populism (see p. 135)? And if it still does, is it not gambling with the future of the nation? Every single paise must be spent on building infrastructure and social security, but it seems that our myopic policies will keep adding to our interest payment numbers year after year and infrastructure and job creation will remain a distant dream. At this time, it is prudent for the government to breach its fiscal deficit numbers and invest massively in infrastructure.

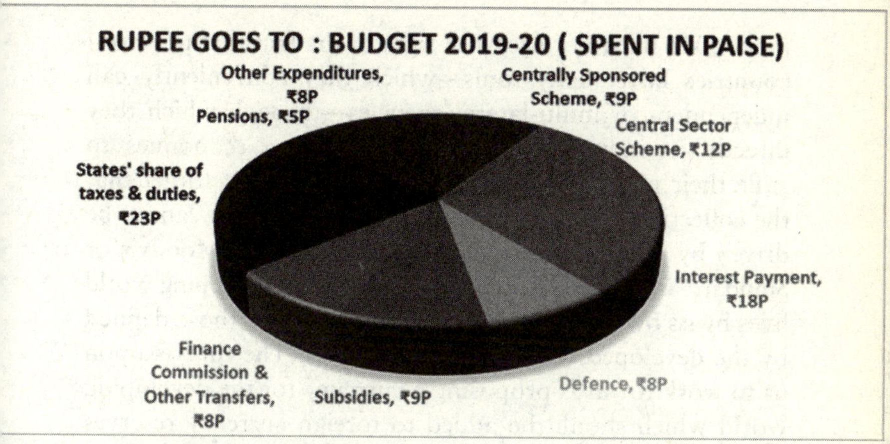

In fact, as long as money is a capital investment towards creating infrastructure, both hard or soft, why should we be worried about a goal like achieving a 3.3 per cent fiscal deficit. The deficit can be 4 per cent, or even 5, but what India needs at present are massive investments to create liveable villages and cities. Once these villages and cities are on their feet, they will repay these investments through enhanced productivity, income-generation, taxes and growth. Why do we suffocate growth by creating an 'investment deficit' and choke growth and keep concentrating on maintaining the fiscal deficit? In my view, prudence lies in tilting the balance and avoiding an investment deficit today to ensure that we have a healthy fiscal deficit tomorrow. The need of the hour is a massive upliftment of basic amenities and it is time that we avoid the prescriptions given to us by the textbook economists of both the International Monetary Fund and the World Bank. We have already paid a heavy price by borrowing economists from the World Bank, the IMF and other leading global forums and universities to guide us. It is now time to look inwards and develop an indigenous growth model. We must not ever lose sight of the fact that powerful countries have many tools—which they conveniently call independent or multi-lateral agencies—through which they directly or indirectly pressurize developing economies to stifle their plans and growth. We must also not forget that the collective future of such a massive population cannot be driven by ratings delivered by agencies such as Moody's or Standard and Poor's. It is important that the developing world lives by its own definitions and criteria and not those defined by the developed world's rating agencies. The time is upon us to work towards proposing a currency for the developing world which should be added to foreign currency reserves and for international trading. Dollar-denominated trading does not work for the developing world. It is time, also, that India takes the lead in creating an organization that works for the developing world, unlike the WTO.

Digital Inclusion

We need a clear and comprehensive vision, and an implementation plan, for digital inclusion to ensure and bolster economic growth and self sufficiency. We cannot become a digitally empowered society, despite having the best technical brains, if we keep using products made and designed in the US, that too by Indians. In the absence of home-grown solutions, we are overpaying for the enterprise of digital inclusion. This issue has to be addressed from the standpoints of all aspects related to digitization—software, hardware and cybersecurity—and every aspect has to be led by Indians, in full knowledge that our digital horizons are expanding into Artificial Intelligence, Machine Learning, 3D Printing, automation and will go beyond what is comprehensible at present. In fact, what people call Artificial Intelligence is, I believe, the real intelligence and is here to stay.

These are a few steps which India must take to ensure universal digital inclusion:

- India needs to move from being a body shop for the world in the digital field to becoming a market and world leader. To achieve this end, we must aim at setting up small and large world-class institutes in every region which plug into larger institutes of excellence across the country. All these must produce the specialized human resources which are needed for the next one or two decades. The academia of these, as well as that of other institutes, should follow a 'revolving door' policy of spending time in the industry via sabbatical or other schemes. This will change the outlook of academics, as well as that of those working in the industry, make them aware of each other's culture and needs, and foster a more cohesive collaboration between academia and the industry.
- Indians cannot remain the best employees in the technical domain. We must become the best employers and entrepreneurs. It is Indian companies which should take the lead in providing solutions in the social-media and networking domains, in automation, as well as cyber security and cyber warfare.
- Digital products and solutions are required for our entire population, and there is no reason why our expenditure in these areas should be remitted to the developed world. We must build our own digital ecosystem. This gains even more urgency in the current climate, where we are enthusiastically talking about building SMART cities.
- Once we are ready with a roadmap, the government must mandate the use of technology in all spheres of

governance and administration. By 2030, India must be a fully digital country where 100 per cent of the public services and interface happens digitally—safely and with cost-effectiveness.
- Elections can also be moved into the digital space, where electronic voting, linked to Aadhaar, will make it possible to enable everyone to vote from the comfort of their homes.

Real digital inclusion will happen only when we have a sound domestic ecosystem for which the world is willing to pay a premium to use. We Indians can do it all by ourselves, all we need is a vision with a bold action plan and with the government playing the role of a key enabler.

Corruption, the Biggest Hindrance to Economic Growth

Despite the existence of institutions such as the Chief Vigilance Commission and the Enforcement Directorate, and rules such as the Right to Information (RTI) Act, bribe seeking, hoarding, black marketing and tax evasion still remain a major cause of delay and deficiency in the delivery of goods and services, and have collectively created a vicious cycle. We must change the system in a few important and fundamental ways to kill the network of corruption, especially among government representatives and functionaries.

- We must bring in a guaranteed service charter for the delivery of each and every government service.
- Reduce artificial barriers like affidavits, or multi-level authorization processes for matters that should be routine. For instance, why should the transfer of a senior staff in a ministry need the approval of a minister? Shouldn't this be carried out as a

straightforward inter-office process? In a similar manner, why should sanction be sought to prosecute a government official for crimes related to bribery and other provisions of the Criminal Procedure Code?

- We need concrete steps to ensure that processes in the government are system dependent and unambiguous, and not subject to interpretation on the whims and fancies of the officials in charge. If the Law Commission of India finds that certain laws have become subject to interpretation and are breeding corruption, they must be amended with participation from citizens.
- No government form should be more than two pages long and, as a thumb rule, no such form should take more than fifteen minutes to fill in, and no approval should move more than three levels. The lengthier and more cumbersome we make processes, the more opportunities arise for bribe-takers to come up and claim to bypass circuitous processes. All interfaces with the government should be hassle-free and the majority of the work processes, and forms, should be available online and on demand.
- No official should be allowed to accept any gift or memento of any kind, and of any value.
- More importantly, it is the bribe-seeker who should be penalized and not the bribe-giver. It is common-sense that no one is willing to part with money unless compelled, and hence it is the bribe-seeker who should be axed. The existing system is heavily tilted in favour of the bribe-seeker, to the extent that it seems as if governmental processes have been geared in such a way that they seek to dissuade the bribe-giver from lodging a complaint. In the eyes of the law, both the

bribe-seeker and bribe-giver are equal offenders, if the incident of bribery is reported after seven days.[98] This state of affairs should be changed so that whenever a transaction with regards to bribery is reported, with evidence, it is only the bribe-seeker who is penalized. Isn't it bizarre that a victim is treated as a criminal? This must be changed. This will go a long way in reporting people who ask for bribes. The Prevention of Corruption (Amendment) Act 2018 needs to be looked at again to ensure that the threshold of punishment is so high that bribe-seekers do not dare to think about bribes or gratification to deliver on their responsibility.

- Also, in cases of deficiency in delivery of services, the senior-most official of the department concerned must be taken to task. For instance, in the case of bad roads, the technical head (the superintending engineer), the officer (in charge of the area as either ward officer or municipal commissioner) and the public representative of the area must be made parties and suitable penalties imposed upon them. Unless we fix accountability and take defaulters to task at the right level, we will keep cursing the system without seeing much impact. At the moment, officers only have authority, divorced from responsibility and accountability. The only punishments they ever get are reprimands, bad press and, at most, a transfer.
- The compensation of government staff should be in two parts, comprising a basic salary and a performance-linked component. Even if we start with a ratio of 90:10, we must begin somewhere and this ratio should become 70: 30 over a period of time.
- Firstly, we must do away with the permission and approval raj—any permits, licenses and business

registrations (if at all needed) should be done at the national level through the DEFA only, reflecting a united and integrated India. There is no reason for businessmen and enterprises to register in each state. They can be included in a comprehensive National Register and the registration fee can then be proportionately shared by the Centre with the state where the enterprise is based. This should be the norm for all vehicle registrations too. This state-level registration is not only a big cause of harassment, but also a breeding ground for corruption. When we speak of a unified, one India, our conduct in the country should reflect that in our experience, in our interface with the government, and its offices.

- As long as the guidelines for a business and profession are clear, why does one need a license, an approval or a no-objection certificate? And, despite all these licenses, approvals and NOCs, and inspectors, the adherence rate is not more than 10 per cent in the best case scenario. We must towards self-declaration, and self-regulation, which is overseen by random and surprise checks with exemplary fines to act as a deterrence for non-compliance. A simple, straightforward way is to have entrepreneurs register their businesses with the DEFA—whether on its app, website or office where they pay fees, at yearly or five-yearly intervals—and drop off the DEFA grid if they change or shut down the business. We must implement all of this else 'ease of doing business' will remain a pious platitude and a distant dream.
- Whistle-blower protection needs a big push, along with a corruption ombudsman in every district, every state, and nationally, to address corruption in the higher echelons of power and administration.

- Administrative agencies, investigative agencies and the judiciary should look at achieving twin objectives: imposing exemplary fines for offences and ensuring that delivery of justice is time-bound. Today, for most offences, the fine is so low that there is actually an incentive to commit a crime and walk away by paying a nominal fine or penalty. Moreover, the delivery of justice is a dream that rarely comes true. An exemplary fine will have two benefits: it will be a deterrent for offenders and it will provide agencies a source of finance for continued functioning and growth. We must learn from the US, where fines imposed on defaulting companies run into the millions and billions of dollars. The same scale of punishments—a substantial fine or a prison sentence, or both—suitably adapted to Indian realities, must be applied.
- I simply cannot understand how corporations in India, crores of rupees in debt, afford rich foundations—disguised mostly as CSR initiatives—and highly paid CEOs? It is time to become realistic. If we are serious about addressing the issue of financial defaults, frauds and bribes, we need the Ministry of Corporate Affairs to create a fraud-prevention intelligence and investigation unit to check early signs of fraud by companies.
- An online platform, provided by the government, and monitored by external agencies, should be used for seeking online donations for election funding. No party should be allowed to collect funds directly from corporates and also, since these funds are either public money or money garnered from the corporates, all political parties must be governed by the RTI Act.

- Citizens should have the option to rate every single government office and the service it provides, either online, or through an app, or at the office premises. They should also be able to offer suggestions and these suggestions should influence at least a part of the salary increment of the staff, and affect their promotions. Only locally registered citizens who have visited an office will be entitled to rate an office or a person. This will change the approach of how office staff deals with citizens. It should also be emphasized that the citizens should act responsibly in rating the officer and the office and there should also be a system in place so that the citizens' identity can be kept secret and they aren't harassed for their honest assessment and feedback.

Loan Waivers and Non-Performing Assets

As discussed earlier, financial doles and farm loan waivers do not bode well for the economy if used as a tool for electoral gains. Both of these must be extraordinary steps, and used purely as an economic strategy to offer relief in extreme conditions. Additionally, banks should be treated not merely as mere financial institutions which seek deposits and give out loans, but as strategic investors who help build businesses. What this calls for is for banks to build expertise in dealing with specific sectors and industries so that all their aspects, as well as risks and benefits are clearly understood. Without this expertise, banks will have to perennially deal with the problem of NPAs. Banks need to redefine themselves and become more relevant to the growing needs of the emerging economy. Each bank must have an investment committee, solely responsible for evaluation of a loan demand, and the final word on the decision. This committee can even become the generator of a small revenue stream, through a management and holding fee which they can charge should the investing company seek continued advice and oversight.

Consumer Protection

In today's age, it is easy for a corporate house, a business entity, or even an individual, to default or commit a wrong and find an easy escape. However, the consumer who ultimately pays for the product or the services has only one mechanism for redressal: the courts. And it is common knowledge how harrowing the experience of attaining legal recourse is, and how long it takes to be delivered. Every citizen of India has, at some point in time or the other, felt fleeced by companies. But it is a simple matter for them to shun responsibility as the government has not done its homework to put appropriate measures to avoid the loot of its citizens. For instance, in the case of bank deposits, the liability of the government is limited to only Rs 1 lakh, irrespective of the quantum of our deposits. Neither is this common knowledge, nor have the consequences of this been properly analysed. A recent example: in the beginning of 2018, the Industrial Development Bank of India (IDBI) was near collapse due to a number of factors and had to be rescued, at the end of the year, by the Life Insurance Corporation of India (LIC). Had my hard-earned savings been invested in IDBI, the entire amount would have been reduced to Rs 1 lakh for no fault of mine. What kind of consumer interest is covered by the country's banking system? Also, this has a deeper impact on the morale of the citizens and weakens our trust in the system.

In the case of consumer goods, if one buys an expensive product, the company may grant a 10-year warranty on a part of the product and not the entire product. When something goes wrong, the consumer has no way of knowing if it was only the part under warranty that was repaired or the company billed the consumer as per its whims. The consumer guidance and protection laws must ensure that beyond a certain price, products should be entirely guaranteed for a particular duration. The rules are, at present, utterly arbitrary. An article that costs Rs 5,000 may have a three-month warranty, and no guarantee; at times it may have neither. Even a cellphone that costs Rs 1 lakh has only a one-year warranty. It is the duty of the government to ensure that a customer who is spending Rs 1 lakh for a commodity has peace of mind, both in terms of service or replacement in case of product failure. It is time to put together a guideline for various price points. So, say a cellphone or any other article costs Rs 20,000. It must come with an inbuilt repair warranty, or a replacement guarantee, for a predefined period. In the case of each article, the company must specify the expected lifespan of the product in its description. If the seller does not have a nationwide network, the customer should not be charged for shipping the product. According to a recently released report, one out five products sold online is fake. Should the government not address this issue?[99]

The quality of voice calls and the speed of data on our mobile telephonic networks are patchy at best. This inspite of the fact that each network loudly advertises its superiority. All these companies use airwaves that are national property, and are leased out to them by the government, but they have no accountability either to consumers or to the government.

If you have travelled to Delhi by air, you must have noticed that, on exiting Terminal 3 and heading to the car park, you will get either soaked by rain or baked by the sun, as the parallel roads have no roofs to serve as shelters. We claim to have built a world-class airport in the National

Capital Region, and for years, this is the plight of the millions of passengers who have travelled to Delhi. This has never become an issue because, I believe, bureaucrats and politicians do not need to use the conventional exits; they simply slip out of the VIP exit, which, needless to say, is well covered.

When travelling abroad, most foreign airlines will not serve you a vegetarian meal. They will simply say that the option does not exist. The world's largest online retailer launched a voice-controlled virtual assistant in India, running on Artificial Intelligence, for Rs 14,999. This assistant does not understand Hindi, even though the company claims it soon will. There's a simple point to be made here—could this company launch the same product in the US if it did not understand English, or in Germany and Japan if it did not understand German or Japanese? Most products marketed and sold by MNCs in India do not carry product descriptions in Hindi. Do the MNCs want us to learn English to understand what they are selling, when they are selling in India? Shouldn't they mention the details in Hindi too? Social media giants as well as internet companies mine data from a large percentage of Indians who currently use their applications and products. We happily host these companies in the country, and even encourage them, but would other countries, especially the large market economies of the US, Europe and UK allow such flagrant exploitation of people's data? It is only in India, where consumer laws are weak and enforcement even weaker, that consumers suffer.

In my opinion, Indian consumers do not really matter to large corporations. They appear to have extensive networks within the government and among officials, and they don't care if consumers suffer as long as their political masters are kept happy. We are merely guinea pigs, and we cannot keep taking false pride in India becoming the third or the fifth largest economy in the world. Even though we form one-sixth of the world's population, and one of the biggest markets for goods and services, we are not actually cared for, leave alone treated with respect. For a large part, it is the Indian government which is responsible for this state of affairs. It has a Ministry of Consumer Affairs which does not take proactive steps to protect Indian consumers or consumers in India. It is time that laws are changed so that when a consumer spends even a single rupee, he or she should get what is promised and expected. India needs a consumer rights protection watchdog that works for consumers and is proactive and effective enough so that it becomes a deterrent to people and organizations working against the rights of the consumers.

The government should ensure that the quality as well as the quantum of products and services being marketed in the country are at par with the best; if a consumer feels cheated, and complains, the seller should be promptly and severely penalized to serve as a deterrent. In fact, why should the government wait for a consumer to complain? Should it not conduct spot inspections, testing and surveys to pre-empt the chances of customers being fleeced by companies? It can institute an intelligence wing tasked with scanning advertisements and claims, and verifying them by random sampling. It goes without saying, also, that the government is a provider of services to its people, and must come under the purview of consumer laws to provide the services it is deemed to provide for, after collecting multiple taxes. A massive revamp and improvement in consumer laws and grievance redressal will be the single biggest change that every Indian will not only appreciate but also never forget.

Governance and Administrative Reforms

It is futile to address any issue without addressing the bedrocks of governance and administration, and equally futile to talk about any worthwhile change. This has to be the overarching theme if we are looking at transforming the nation.

There are a number of areas in which reforms are not only required, but are vital.

Members of Parliament (MPs): We are still following the system of parliamentary representation with 550 MPs, based on the 1970 census, when the population of India was 54.8 crores. Then, almost half a century ago, each MP represented a population of 10 lakh in Parliament and today, when the population has more than doubled, the total number represented is about 24 lakh. How can a single MP represent 24 lakh people? Is it not time to reconsider the number of seats in Parliament so that the population per MP is manageable? The fact remains that any readjustment in the number of constituencies cannot be undertaken until 2026, in keeping with the Constitution (Amendment) Act 2002, but are we being fair to our MPs, or to the people they represent?

It is also urgent that the parameters on which an MP can be independently and transparently assessed be defined and they need more training in policy and execution. With these measures in place, the MPs, the real law makers of the country, will deliver that for which they are sent by the electorate to the Parliament. The issue of creating and maintaining clear indicators becomes even more important because even though the quality of ministers is majorly decided by the 'electorate' through the Lok Sabha, key portfolios are being held by MPs from the Rajya Sabha. Each minister should ideally present a performance scorecard which should include, among others: new initiatives taken, delivery of programmes through number of lives touched—including, but not limited to, actual fund utilization for beneficiaries (as part of the funds are absorbed in travel, administration and office infrastructure)—resolution of grievances, surprise visits undertaken, and action taken against non-performers and corrupt officials. We can keep adding parameters, but the important point is to ensure that ministers are not mere figureheads who blindly sign documents presented to them by bureaucrats. Today, bureaucrats prevail upon ministers in almost everything; but if the ministers knew their subject well and did their homework, bureaucratic logjams and redtape could be speedily reduced and the country could fast-track development. The only way in which this would work is for the message to come directly from the Prime Minister. It is solely the responsibility of the PM to allocate work to his colleagues in the cabinet and the ministers of state. Most of the ministers of state have no direct responsibility except presenting papers in the Parliament and cutting ribbons at inaugurations. If this does not change, we will be wasting precious resources. Finally, the public should start rating the performance of ministries and ministers. If citizens' lives are touched and the work accomplished is visible on ground, it is the public which is in the best position to decide who performed and how, and who failed to deliver. This public rating should be institutionalized for every minister, ministry and government office, and must be run by an independent agency in a transparent manner.

However, along with expectation of good performance, each MP must be provided with enough support staff and budgets to ensure that they serve the huge number of people they represent in the august house.

Convergence of Departments: A number of ministries and departments should be merged because we currently have a strange system which operates in silos. Here are a few classic examples: Nutrition (under the ICDS scheme) is under the Ministry of Women and Child Development; pharmaceuticals and medical devices are under the Ministry of Chemicals and Fertilizers, while other aspects related to health are looked after by the Ministry of Health and Family Welfare. Employee State Insurance Corporation (ESIC) Hospitals come under the Ministry of Labour while the Ex-Servicemen Contributory Health Scheme (ECHS) comes under the Ministry of Defence. There are at least twenty-six ministries which handle matters related to health.

The Ministry of Human Resource Development, the Ministry of Culture and the Ministry of Skill Development and Entrepreneurship are three different ministries. Isn't the mandate of MHRD also the development of skills and the promotion of culture? Would it not make more sense to include entrepreneurship under the Ministry of Micro, Small and Medium Enterprises?

How can rural development happen without agriculture? Should not the ministries of Agriculture and Rural Development be merged? This merger could seed the overarching dream of the development of rural India, with a focus on agriculture.

In fact, what would make most sense is to converge ministries with a broader mandate under a single cabinet minister, adding more ministers of state who would shoulder the responsibility, along with their cabinet colleague, of creating and achieving a larger vision for the country in that particular sector. Without these convergences, there is bound to be infighting, and work that happens in exclusive silos. These will prevent things from happening and the country will suffer from slow growth.

Rules and Regulations: All rules and regulations must be simple, unambiguous and easy to understand. This will go a long way in taking away the largely arbitrary power of discretion from the administrative machinery, which must only be entrusted with execution and service delivery on behalf of the government. Ideally, no government policy document should be more than fifteen pages long and no form more than two pages. Rules and regulations must be system driven so that they do not need committees to ponder over and ratify them. For instance, all increases in income and taxes should be linked to inflation data, with a predefined formula. Also, all rules must be reviewed and changed with time; ideally, once every decade.

All government departments should have a digital dashboard which indicates how many beneficiaries connected with them per month. Similarly, every scheme of the government must have a digital dashboard, updated live, which will show the number of beneficiaries, funds allocated, funds disbursed and funds utilized.

Most importantly, artificial barriers are uncalled for in today's age and need to be done away with. These barriers include demands such as asking for bank drafts that are issued only by nationalized banks; affidavits which must be attested by notaries public; documents which need to be attested, either by gazetted officers or other authorities; demands made for proofs of identity and residence, among others. We must trust and respect our citizens. We must build our systems in such a way that there are inbuilt checks and balances, and information is not only readily available but also private and protected. The removal of barriers will only make the life of citizens easier.

The governments, both at the Centre and the states, should create unified portals www.publicopinion.gov.in or www.opinion.gov.in, so that people will not have to wade through multiple government websites to figure out which document or issue is put in the public domain for comments and suggestions. This will ensure that people become active participants in governance by sharing their views on important government bills, acts and documents. Also, though this might be a little too much to expect, the best and brightest ideas received from the public should be recognized so that people are motivated to participate in the processes of policy making and reform.

Bureaucracy

We cannot run a 21st-century government with an administrative setup that dates back to the 18th century. India has suffered immensely from its outdated administrative setup and the poor governance which results from it. In reality, the whole system is crumbling and regressive. This situation has not changed even in the last few years, despite a technocratic and bold Prime Minister at the helm. If we are aiming to transform governance and the administration, we must be sure of one thing: the bureaucracy will resist all measures which will bring in transparency and accountability, as bureaucrats love authority but hate accountability. Moreover, if we entrust the bureaucracy with correcting itself, no major change will ever happen. Therefore, it is the Prime Minister himself who will have to find a 'close team' that can deliver this as a reform. If major bureaucratic reforms are carried out, they will need a nod from Parliament and will be sufficient to demonstrate the commitment of the government as well as the maturity of our lawmakers. Without these, there can be no meaningful change in India. Once these plans of reform are formulated, we need speed, efficiency and effectiveness in our entire chain of command to implement them.

The primary goals of the reforms are a system in which interfacing with the government will not mean interference on its part; where communications with the government will not take on the tone of insults; and getting work done in the government will not become harassment. We need a complete overhaul in the system, a shift in culture and mindset which will change the bureaucracy from its administrative role to a service-oriented one, where they serve citizens, making life more convenient for us and enhancing our prosperity. This calls for a massive cultural change, along with changes in systems of delivery and performance evaluation. We must remember that while accountability can be tracked with systems, it must be enforced with the relevant work culture. Without a genuine change in culture and mindset, people will find a way to circumvent any system and make it dysfunctional.

The following crises in our bureaucracy are crucial, in my opinion, and need addressing to make it more effective and bring it in tune with the needs of the day:

- The elite examination which governs entry into the civil services.
- The current performance appraisal system of Annual Confidential Reports (ACRs)—since ACRs are written by bureaucrats for bureaucrats, the norm is to 'do no harm'. People are generally rated between 8-10 in their ACRs, and the pattern continues year after year, batch after batch. They have now become meaningless.

- The present-day approach of bureaucrats: to 'control' and 'govern' and not to 'work as a team' for 'development'. Also, most officials work in silos, and for themselves, governed by their egos and, at times, petty impulses which may pit one official against the other. With this attitude, there can never be a team approach in whatever they do.
- Bureaucrats are more 'procedure driven' than 'outcome driven' which is why files routinely take months to travel from one desk to another. If we expect major improvements in delivery with such an approach, they will not happen. The bureaucracy must be service oriented, accountable and outcome driven.

Therefore, we need the following major changes:

- The first major transformation is that the entrance examination for civil services should be scrapped or phased out and only specialists who have the relevant degree of knowledge or work experience in a particular department should be inducted into it. For example, a primary schoolteacher, based on her qualification, experience and outstanding achievements, should have a shot at becoming Secretary, Education. In the same way, a nurse, health worker, physiotherapist, pharmacist or a doctor should have a chance at running a district health administration and even become the Secretary, Health. If the departments of Defence and Science and Technology have never depended on the Indian Administrative Services to run them, and delivered good results, why are we running other departments with officers with no domain expertise?

- Lateral entry and lateral exit should be made an integral part of the administrative (bureaucratic) system.
- The training pattern of bureaucrats, and the Central Civil Services rules must be modified to reflect the needs of a transitioning country.
- All public officers must get feedback and ratings from actual users, with details.
- Every official must disclose the direct cost to the government, which includes the cost of his office, including his dedicated staff, trainings in India and abroad, so that the public knows how much money is being spent by the government on an official to serve the public.
- As of now, we have an appraisal system that looks at ACRs, which only factor an individual's performance. We must move from the ACR system to the CPR (Comprehensive Performance Review) system.

The CPR should include:

- An Individual Performance Review (IPR), which will be based on yearly goals or assigned deliverables, to be decided by the head of the department. This chain should be followed, down the line, for every government employee whether permanent or contractual. Soft skills, especially in the handling of the public, must be integral part of the training, and a key criterion in the assessment of performance. The following weightages within the IPR will ensure even closer attention to detail:
    - Defining time-bound quantifiable and measurable deliverables (15 per cent)

- Completion of targets within the proposed time frame (15 per cent)
- Completion of targets without increase in budgets (15 per cent)
- Utilization of funds (15 per cent)
- Disposal of files and grievances (10 per cent)
- Innovations (15 per cent)
- Customer service feedback from the citizens who interfaced with the officer (15 per cent)
- The weightage should be objectively apportioned for any misses in achieving targets.

• An annual Department Performance Review (DPR), in which an assessment of a department's performance, based on the goals set for the year, is conducted. This review should also include a service and delivery feedback mechanism to assess if citizens are being treated with respect or ill handled. The individual weightages for the DPR are as follows:

- Identifying key annual deliverables and priorities, to be done by the minister in-charge and officers up to the rank of Joint Secretary (15 per cent)
- The completion of pre-set targets within the time frame (15 per cent)
- The achievement of targets without an increase in budgets (15 per cent)
- Full, and judicious utilization of funds (15 per cent)
- The disposal of grievances (15 per cent)
- Feedback from the people who interfaced with the department for work (15 per cent)

• A Government Performance Review (GPR), which is an overall performance rating of the government based on feedback from a public survey taken from citizens for all the departments and ministries, whether in the district, the states, or at the Centre. All the metrics which form the basis of performance must be based on actual verifiable data. The following weightages are key to assess performance:

- The implementation of key announcements versus the goals achieved in terms of beneficiaries or actual lives touched (10 per cent)
- Ensuring that inflation targets are met, and the prices of essential products controlled (10 per cent)
- Keeping the fiscal deficit under control (10 per cent)
- Ensuring the development and growth of the country (10 per cent)
- The utilization of funds and achieving an increase in the number of beneficiaries of schemes (10 per cent weightage)
- Achieving a reduction in poverty (10 per cent)
- Increase in GDP per capita or an alternative indicator (10 per cent)
- The disposal of grievances (10 per cent)
- As with any other provider of services, feedback from the ultimate consumers is crucial. The government must work for public welfare, and if the work done by the government is visible on the ground and felt by the public, it must also be judged by the public. Hence, genuine feedback should have a weightage of 20 per cent. This feedback can be made via Interactive Voice Response (IVR) system, or some other suitable mechanism it is not misused.

- To calculate the overall CPR of individual officers, the IPR should be allocated 40 per cent; the DPR 30 per cent and the GPR 30 per cent.
- The CPR can be implemented from the level of the Secretary and move downwards in a phased manner in the next five years. Till this reform on performance is done, bureaucrats will remain in 'sleep mode' as their retirement age is fixed and they, in a real sense, don't bother about the government of the day or its vision or programmes.
- It goes without saying that the CPR should not have any reservation or weightage for any category and be based strictly on merit and performance that have been transparently and objectively assessed.

Modifying the Tenured System

While job security is a wonderful thing, and enshrined within the terms of employment, it is also the biggest bane of bureaucracy. We must modify the system, keeping job security centrestage, but only for those officers who have performed well and have been judged through a transparent appraisal system. If the government is serious about a 'Big Change', the first major reform is bureaucracy and the rest can wait.

All officers of head of department rank (starting from district magistrates) must be put on a five-year contract term, based on a review of their performance, with decent financial incentives to award outstanding work. On the other hand, if they fail to live up to a minimum IPR of 80 per cent for three years out of a five-year term, they must be relieved from service. Good performance should be the sole criteria to decide seniority, despite the fact that the term of employment is contractual. All pay hikes and promotions should be based on the CPR and the financial incentives for good performance should be at par with the best in any other sector and should add to their service record.

As a corollary, no official or minister should be allowed to travel business class. This is sheer wastage of public money, which can otherwise be used for productive investment.

Also, for every middle- and senior-level position, there should be a clearly defined succession plan. The officer-designate will also chip in as and when needed, so that delivery of services is not affected.

eOffice and eFile Systems: No file pertaining to government work should pass more than three levels, and each level should not take more than a week. If more information is required for a decision, or time, this needs to be noted on the file with a proper justification. Moving the filing system online will allow officials more mobility, since they can access them from either handheld devices, or laptops. This will free them up so that at least 20 per cent of their time is spent in the field, meeting and interacting with the people whom they serve. Moving the decision-making process online will another significant impact. It will curtail verbal orders and decision-making. No verbal instructions should be allowed at any level; they should only be issued online.

Data

Data is our weakest link as far as policy making or analysis are concerned. In conducting research for this book, I could not find a go-to source which would provide me data on India—among others, the number of jobs, the number of loans disbursed to individuals or to industries, the number of people in the middle class, the number of farmers, the number of retailers. How can one plan for the country in the absence of data and based on census figures from 2011?

The government must leverage the Digital India programme to ensure that population wise and sectoral data are available and updated live. This is one of the biggest drawbacks in planning—that data is not available, and if available, it is old and patchy and full of discrepancies. A website, https://data.gov.in was launched by the government but the data for key indicators is census based and dates back to 2011, which is of little use for drafting policies for today.

A Citizen's Charter

How many citizens know what they are expected to do and what not? Ironically, even seven decades after Independence, India still does not have a 'Citizen's Charter' and it is time that the government comes out with one which will tell what a citizen of India should expect from the government and what is expected of him and her. This will ensure that not only are the 'rights of the citizen of India' clearly defined, but also the 'duties of the citizen of India'. These duties should include clearly mentioned dos and don'ts and should be legally enforceable. Without discharging our duties, we cannot expect the government to deliver its best. At the same time, when rights and duties are clearly defined, both are expected to stick to their roles and deliver on them. Ideally, this should become a part of the Constitution of India, like the Directive Principles of State Policy.

Cultural Policy

Culture is the foundation of a democratic society. Indian civilization is as old as human history and has survived multiple invasions and natural disasters. Yet, despite having such a glorious past and rich heritage, India still lacks a cultural policy. In this context, it is pertinent to note what

UNESCO states: 'The cultural and creative industries are among the fastest growing sectors in the world. With an estimated global worth of 4.3 trillion USD per year, the culture sector now accounts for 6.1% of the global economy. They generate annual revenues of US$ 2,250 billion and nearly 30 million jobs worldwide, employing more people aged 15 to 29 than any other sector. The cultural and creative industries have become essential for inclusive economic growth, reducing inequalities and achieving the goals set out in the 2030 Sustainable Development Agenda.'[100]

Given the enormous contribution which culture can make to the economy, and to employment, it is surprising that though India has a Ministry of Culture, it still does not have a cultural policy. Considering that a cultural policy will support the creation, production, distribution of and access to cultural goods and services, i.e. a creative economy, India should set up a team to draft the cultural policy of India in a time-bound manner. In this India can perhaps take lessons from Germany which has had a focussed approach on a culture policy since the nineteenth century.

The Implementation Frame-work and a Vision for India

Having worked on drafting policies for a decade and being part of the government afterwards, I have seen how even the best policies fail. The twin problems policies face are interpretation and implementation. Bureaucrats interpret policies to suit their needs, and the less said about implementation the better. Therefore, all the points mentioned above have to be broken down into implementation blocks for each component and a roadmap developed, time bound and with all the resources needed to achieve the milestone-based deliverables with performance based dashboards that are transparently posted in the public domain by each implementing department. The performance must also be reviewed monthly at the ministerial level.

Converting Policies into Programmes

Once a policy is framed, the respective department involved in converting the policy challenges and directions into programmes must:

- Assess the challenges and the root cause for the challenges in each sector.
- Formulate a vision for each sector before delving into the details for each sectoral plan.
- Create guiding principles or filters through which each recommendation must pass through. Each recommendation has to be citizen centric and improve the quality of life; it must balance economic contribution and ensure job creation; increase productivity and improve quality; be eco-friendly, simple and hassle free.
- Ensure resource assessment in planning for each recommendation.
- Clearly spell out the implementation framework, along with the monitoring and evaluation framework.

It is a fact that some policies and programmes need to be reoriented to changing realities and times and that should be done as per the findings of an independent audit conducted by an agency along the lines of the Comptroller and Auditor General of India. Such a body should be set up by an act of Parliament and the report of the implementation should be laid out in every session of the parliament with equal representation from the ruling and other parties.

There will be state subjects, but respective states must bring in legislation to handle the issues at their respective levels with similar agencies to monitor and audit implementation based on milestone-based deliverables. States that have an outstanding performance should be incentivised with more financial aid and officers that do an outstanding job should be given out of turn promotions and substantial financial incentives.

Vision

As a country, as a state, as a district we must have a defined vision and goal for each district, state, sector, the country itself, before deciding what we wish to accomplish. Earlier, India was known as the centre of the world's trading power as well as a powerhouse in terms of educational and scientific knowledge. Now, all that is gone into history, but we need to define what we stand for or what we would like India to be known for? This needs a nationwide debate and a long-term plan. By simply chanting that India will become a 'Vishwa Guru', the Teacher of the World, India will not become a Vishwa Guru.

All developed countries such as the US, UK, the UAE have a 'China Town' in every prominent city. This did not happen suddenly and was the result of long-term vision and planning by China. Now, China has embarked on another long-term plan with the OBOR—the One Belt-One Road Initiative to become a global superpower that will replace the US. Just as China makes its plans decades in advance, India must work on a vision for the next quarter, or even half century, not to become a superpower but a prosperous nation with happy citizens.

To me, as a policy maker, the following, focussing on which we will be able to achieve happy results, are the important constituents of this vision:

- ✓ Empowered women—Vibrant India
- ✓ Cheerful farmers—Progressive India
- ✓ Educated and financially strong youth—Strong India
- ✓ Well-equipped soldiers—Safe and Secure India
- ✓ Empowered consumers and effective governance—Happy India

These are overarching themes.

The government, while drafting a vision, will have to prioritize amongst a lot of competing needs and the priority must be clear.

1. Governance and administrative reforms
2. Distributed growth model
3. Infrastructure
4. Health
5. Education

A Call to Action

Your priority, now that you have read the book, is to think about the areas and sectors in which you would like to see a change. Once you have thought about them, hold discussions among your friends, colleagues, or with a wider audience. And once you have achieved clarity, draft your recommendations and send them to political parties via email or in the form of letters.

Use social media to intelligently and widely highlight issues and your suggestions to address them. Write a blog. Start a petition on www.change.org.

Initiate online communities or an NGO to take forward your agenda for change.

Make use of the RTI Act to check actions taken on your complaint or suggestions and keep following up.

File a PIL (Public Interest Litigation) if the issue can be addressed by a judicial intervention.

Don't forget to vote, even if your choice is NOTA.

And, lastly, never ever give up. This is a system built with your money and is supposed to serve you.

Notes

Policies and How They Impact Us

1. Goyal, Malini, 'India's Problem Is to Find Jobs for 10-12 million New Workers Every Year.' *The Economic Times*, September 2016, https://economictimes.indiatimes.com/opinion/interviews/indias-problem-is-to-find-jobs-for-10-12-million-new-workers-every-year-akshay-kothari-linkedin-india/articleshow/53998506.cms.
2. Kim, Jim Yong, 'Speech by World Bank President Jim Yong Kim: The World Bank Group's Mission: To End Extreme Poverty', October 2016, http://www.worldbank.org/en/news/speech/2016/10/03/speech-by-world-bank-president-jim-yong-kim-the-world-bank-groups-mission-to-end-extreme-poverty.
3. World Bank, 'India: Human Capital Index Rank 115 Out of 157.' October 2018, http://databank.worldbank.org/data/download/hci/HCI_2pager_IND.pdf.
4. Chakravarti, Chaitali, Sagar Malviya, 'Amazon Goes Shopping for Future Retail, to Buy 9.5% Stake.' *The Economic Times*, November 2018, https://economictimes.indiatimes.com/industry/services/retail/amazon-goes-shopping-for-future-retail-to-buy-9-5-stake/articleshow/66504698.cms.
5. Gupta, Soumya, 'Amazon Buys 5% Equity in Shoppers Stop for Rs 179.25 Crore.' *Livemint*, September 2017, https://www.livemint.com/Companies/tkpaE0FHd4i05WmrCo14vM/Amazon-to-invest-Rs17925-crore-in-Shoppers-Stop.html.
6. 'Samara Capital-Amazon Acquire Kumar Mangalam Birla's More Supermarket Chain.' *Business Today*, September 2018, https://www.businesstoday.in/current/corporate/samara-capital-amazon-acquire-kumar-mangalam-birla-more-supermarket-chain/story/282578.html.
7. India Population, https://countrymeters.info/en/India.
8. 'Air Pollution and Child Health: Prescribing Clean Air.' Geneva: World Health Organization, 2018, https://www.who.int/ceh/publications/air-pollution-child-health/en/.
9. 'How Safe Are Your Deposits if Your Bank Fails? Read about the Bail-in Option.', *The Economic Times*, December 2017, https://economictimes.indiatimes.com/industry/banking/

finance/banking/how-safe-are-your-deposits-if-your-bank-fails-read-about-the-bail-in-option/articleshow/61889538.cms

10. 'Land Bill: Govt to Withdraw Key Changes.' *Financial Express*, August 2015, https://www.financialexpress.com/economy/land-bill-govt-to-withdraw-key-changes/113344/.
11. 'Government Rolls Back Restrictions on Withdrawal of Provident Fund.' *The Economic Times*, April 2016, https://economictimes.indiatimes.com/articleshow/51896900.cms?utm_source=contentofinterest&utm_medium=text&utm_campaign=cppst Full PF withdrawal before age of 58 difficult in most cases
12. Ibid.
13. 'No restrictions on WhatsApp, Facebook? Modi Government Withdraws Draft Encryption Policy.' *The Economic Times*, September 2015, https://economictimes.indiatimes.com/tech/internet/no-restrictions-on-whatsapp-facebook-modi-government-withdraws-draft-encryption-policy/articleshow/49057581.cms.
14. Nanda, Prashant K., 'Govt Withdraws Circular on Good Governance Day.' *Livemint*, December 2014, https://www.livemint.com/Politics/9DTeAuCaxomkOShIQHQXcK/Govt-withdraws-circular-on-Good-Governance-Day.html.
15. 'Govt Rolls Back Excise Duty on Gold Jewellery.' *The Hindu Business Line*, May 2012, https://www.thehindubusinessline.com/markets/gold/govt-rolls-back-excise-duty-on-gold-jewellery/article20430578.ece1.
16. 'Rollback Sarkar: Five Decisions that Modi Govt Went Back On.' *Hindustan Times*, April 2016, https://www.hindustantimes.com/india/roll-back-sarkar-five-decisions-that-modi-govt-went-back-on/story-B9SZeYAulFia38NpwqptEP.html.
17. Ibid.
18. Ibid.
19. 'Modi Govt Makes a U-Turn, Withdraws Proposal to Create Social Media Hub.' TheWire.in, August 2018, https://thewire.in/government/modi-govt-makes-a-u-turn-withdraws-proposal-to-create-social-media-hub.
20. Mondal, Dipak, 'One Year of GST: Tax Base Increase to Complex Return Filing System; the Successes and the Failures.' *Business Today*, July 2018,

https://www.businesstoday.in/current/economy-politics/one-year-of-gst-tax-base-increase-to-complex-return-filing-system-find-out-the-successes-and-the-failures/story/279764.html.

21. Rao, Prianka, 'Parliament as a Law Making Body: Background Note for the Conference of Effective Legislatures'. http://www.prsindia.org/administrator/uploads/general/1417684398~~Parliament%20as%20a%20Law%20Making%20Body.pdf
22. Dutta, Prabhash K., 'Did BJP Lose Madhya Pradesh to Nota and Not Congress?' *India Today*, December 2018, https://www.indiatoday.in/elections/story/madhya-pradesh-nota-assembly-seats-bjp-congress-1408724-2018-12-13.

Policies That Will Drive India beyond 2019 and Make it Future Ready

23. Dikshit, Ashutosh, 'Old Age Dependency Ratio Getting Worse in India Underlining Need to Save for Retirement.' *The Economic Times*, October 2013, https://economictimes.indiatimes.com/wealth/plan/old-age-dependency-ratio-getting-worse-in-india-underlining-need-to-save-for-retirement/articleshow/66049594.cms.
24. Searchinger, Tim et al., 'Achieving Replacement Level Fertility: Creating a Sustainable Food Future, Installment Three.' Washington D.C.: World Resources Institute, August 2013, https://www.wri.org/publication/achieving-replacement-level-fertility
25. 'A Future That Works: Automation, Employment and Productivity.' McKinsey Global Institute, January 2017, https://www.mckinsey.com/~/media/mckinsey/featured%20insights/Digital%20Disruption/Harnessing%20automation%20for%20a%20future%20that%20works/MGI-A-future-that-works-Executive-summary.ashx.
26. Shah, Ronak, 'Updated with New Pics: Tata Harrier Full Images Out: Here's How the Hyundai Creta Rival Looks Like.' *Financial Express*, October 2018, https://www.financialexpress.com/auto/car-news/finally-tata-harrier-full-images-out-heres-how-the-harrier-looks-like/1366696/.
27. Kim, Jim Yong, 'Speech by World Bank President Jim Yong Kim: The World Bank Group's Mission: To End Extreme Poverty', October 2016.

28. Beyer, Robert Carl Meyer, 'Jobless Growth?' Washington D.C.: The World Bank, September 2018, http://documents.worldbank.org/curated/en/825921524822907777/Jobless-growth.
29. 'Niti Aayog Strategy Document Estimates 8% Average GDP Growth During 2018-23.' *The Economic Times*, December 2018, https://economictimes.indiatimes.com/news/economy/indicators/niti-aayog-strategy-document-estimates-8-average-gdp-growth-during-2018-23/articleshow/67160030.cms.
30. Mukherjee, Writankar, 'Vivo Plans to Invest Over Rs 4,000 Crore in India.' *The Economic Times*, November 2018, https://economictimes.indiatimes.com/tech/hardware/vivo-plans-to-invest-over-rs-4000-crore-in-india/articleshow/66871796.cms.
31. Khan, Arshad, 'Samsung Opens World's Largest Phone Factory in India; to Create 2,000 Jobs.' *The New Indian Express*, July 2018, http://www.newindianexpress.com/business/2018/jul/09/samsung-opens-worlds-largest-phone-factory-in-india-to-create-2000-jobs-1840695.html.
32. 'IKEA Signs MoU with Uttar Pradesh Govt, Heads to Noida.' *The Indian Express*, December 2018, https://indianexpress.com/article/business/companies/ikea-signs-mou-with-uttar-pradesh-govt-heads-to-noida-5501273/.
33. 'Total Expenditure for the Fiscal Year 2018-19 Is Estimated to Be Over Rs 24.42 Lakh Crore.' New Delhi: Press Information Bureau, Government of India, February 2018, http://pib.nic.in/newsite/PrintRelease.aspx?relid=176044.
34. 'India's Debt Up 50% to Rs 82 Lakh Crore in Modi Era.' *The Economic Times*, January 2019, http://economictimes.indiatimes.com/articleshow/67593687.cms?utm_source=contentofinterest&utm_medium=text&utm_campaign=cppst.
35. 'Total Expenditure for the Fiscal Year 2018-19 Is Estimated to Be Over Rs 24.42 Lakh Crore.' New Delhi: Press Information Bureau, Government of India, February 2018.
36. 'Indian Healthcare Industry Analysis.' New Delhi: India Brand Equity Foundation, 2019, https://www.ibef.org/industry/healthcare-presentation.
37. Ibid.
38. 'Facts and Figures 2016–17.' New Delhi: Indian Railways, 2017, http://www.indianrailways.gov.in/railwayboard/

uploads/directorate/stat_econ/IRSP_2016-17/Facts_Figure/Fact_Figures%20English%202016-17.pdf.
39. 'Tourism and Hospitality Industry in India.' New Delhi: India Brand Equity Foundation, 2019, https://www.ibef.org/industry/tourism-hospitality-india.aspx.
40. 'Employment Prospects in India's IT Sector: Robust Outlook.' New Delhi: Press Information Bureau, Government of India, May 2017, http://pib.nic.in/newsite/PrintRelease.aspx?relid=162046.
41. 'ITeS and IT Companies in India.' New Delhi: India Brand Equity Foundation, https://www.ibef.org/industry/information-technology-india/showcase.
42. 'A BFSI Career: Prospects and Essential Skills.' *India Today*, December 2016, https://www.indiatoday.in/education-today/jobs-and-careers/story/bfsi-career-prospects-360152-2016-12-29
43. Doval, Pankaj, 'Mukesh Ambani Has "Good News" for Mobiles Users, "Bad News" for Airtel, Vodafone Idea.' *Gadgets Now*, October 2018, https://www.gadgetsnow.com/articleshow/66373741.cms?utm_source=toiweb&utm_medium=referral&utm_campaign=toiweb_hptopnews)&utm_source=contentofinterest&utm_medium=text&utm_campaign=cppst.
44. 'Indian Film Industry.' http://www.indianmirror.com/indian-industries/film.html.
45. 'Indian Retail Industry: From Potential to Performance.' ETRetail.com, June 2017, https://retail.economictimes.indiatimes.com/news/industry/-indian-retail-industry-from-potential-to-performance/59141590.
46. 'Educational Statistics at a Glance.' New Delhi, Ministry of Human Resource Development, Government of India, 2016, http://mhrd.gov.in/sites/upload_files/mhrd/files/statistics/ESG2016_0.pdf.
47. 'Yoga Pants Billion Dollar Industry.' Bloomberg.com, November 2018, https://www.bloomberg.com/news/videos/2018-10-31/yoga-pants-billion-dollar-industry-video.
48. 'Kumbh to Generate Rs 1.2 Lakh Crore Revenue: CII.' *The Economic Times*, January 2019, https://economictimes.indiatimes.com/news/economy/indicators/kumbh-to-generate-rs-1-2-lakh-crore-revenue-cii/articleshow/67609608.cms.

49. Khan, Danish, 'Google Admits to Putting Old UIDAI Helpline Number on Your Phone Contact List.' *The Economic Times*, August 2018, https://economictimes.indiatimes.com/news/politics-and-nation/uidai-row-google-says-it-inadvertently-coded-the-number/articleshow/65264353.cms.
50. 'Fines and Penalties.' https://www.gdpreu.org/compliance/fines-and-penalties/
51. Noorden, Richard Van, 'India by the Numbers: Highs and Lows in the Country's Research Landscape.' *Nature*, vol. 521, issue 7551, May 2015, https://www.nature.com/news/india-by-the-numbers-1.17519.
52. Ibid.
53. Ibid.
54. 'Post Office Network,' https://www.indiapost.gov.in/VAS/Pages/AboutUs/PostOfficeNetwork.aspx.
55. 'Direct Selling Companies in India Set to Generate Nearly 2 Crore Jobs by 2025.' Etnownews.com, September 2018, https://www.timesnownews.com/business-economy/companies/article/direct-selling-companies-in-india-set-to-generate-nearly-2-crore-jobs-by/278175.
56. 'Australian Economy Enters 27th Year of Recession-free Growth.', June 2018, https://www.reuters.com/article/us-australia-economy-gdp-instantview/australian-economy-enters-27th-year-of-recession-free-growth-idUSKCN1J206K.

The Critical Sectors

57. 'India: Human Capital Index Rank 115 out of 157.' Washington D.C.: World Bank, October 2018, http://databank.worldbank.org/data/download/hci/HCI_2pager_IND.pdf.
58. 'Age Structure and Marital Status.' Ministry of Home Affairs, Government of India, http://censusindia.gov.in/Census_And_You/age_structure_and_marital_status.aspx.
59. 'Gaming Disorder.' World Health Organization, https://www.who.int/features/qa/gaming-disorder/en/.
60. 'WHO Certifies Sri Lanka Malaria-free.' World Health Organization, http://www.searo.who.int/mediacentre/releases/2016/1631/en/.
61. 'India: Human Capital Index Rank 115 out of 157.' Washington D.C.: World Bank, October 2018.

62. 'Transforming Science and Technology in India.' *Economic Survey 2017–18*. New Delhi: Ministry of Finance, Government of India, p. 120, http://mofapp.nic.in:8080/economicsurvey/pdf/119-130_Chapter_08_ENGLISH_Vol_01_2017-18.pdf.
63. 'Research and Development in India.' India Brand Equity Foundation, June 2017, https://www.ibef.org/industry/research-development-india.aspx.
64. 'India Has 14 Out of 15 Most Polluted Cities in the World.' *The Times of India*, May 2018, https://timesofindia.indiatimes.com/world/india-has-14-out-of-15-most-polluted-cities-in-the-world-/articleshow/63997961.cms.
65. 'Air Pollution and Child Health: Prescribing Clean Air.' World Health Organization, 2018, https://www.who.int/ceh/publications/air-pollution-child-health/en/.
66. 'World Bank Country and Lending Groups.' Washington D.C. World Bank, https://datahelpdesk.worldbank.org/knowledgebase/articles/906519.
67. 'No Plans to Grant Most Favoured Nation Status to India, Says Pakistan Government.' *Hindustan Times*, November 2018, https://www.hindustantimes.com/world-news/no-plans-to-grant-most-favoured-nation-status-to-india-says-pakistan-government/story-kqwDh1S4pZ2UogwLu4Sy6M.html.
68. 'Preparedness of Armed Forces: Defence Production and Procurement.' New Delhi: Ministry of Defence, July 2018, http://164.100.47.193/lsscommittee/Estimates/16_Estimates_29.pdf.
69. Rajawat, K Yatish, 'Farmers Suffer While Leaders Have a Field Day.' DNA, October 2018, https://www.dnaindia.com/india/report-dna-opinion-farmers-suffer-while-leaders-have-a-field-day-2671335.
70. 'Agriculture in India: Information about Indian Agriculture and Its Importance.' India Brand Equity Foundation, October 2018, https://www.ibef.org/industry/agriculture-india.aspx.
71. Nair, Remya, 'Over 50 % Agricultural Households Are Facing Indebtedness: Nabard.' Livemint, February 2019, https://www.livemint.com/Industry/CYMrgvxGIVnCreNooCAo1K/Over-50-of-agricultural-households-in-debt-Nabard.html.
72. 'Socio Economic and Caste Census 2011.' Government of India, https://secc.gov.in/reportlistContent.
73. 'Some Characteristics of Agricultural Households in India.'

Ministry of Statistics and Programme Implementation, Government of India, 2013, http://mospi.nic.in/sites/default/files/publication_reports/Report_569_4dec15_1.pdf.

74. Sirohi, Naresh, 'To Double the Farmer's Income: A Promise.' Delhi: Jebu Research Private Limited, 2018.
75. Ibid.
76. Ibid.
77. Roy, Vijay C., 'Punjab Facing Stagnancy in Agriculture: State's Economic Survey.' *Business Standard* , May 2013, https://www.business-standard.com/article/economy-policy/punjab-facing-stagnancy-in-agriculture-state-s-economic-survey-113033000131_1.html.
78. Khanday, Zulufkar Ahmad, Akram, Mohammad, 'Health Status of Marginalized Groups in India.' *International Journal of Applied Sociology* 2012, vol. 2, issue 6, pp. 60-70, https://www.researchgate.net/publication/272768249_Health_Status_of_Marginalized_Groups_in_India/download.
79. 'Elderly in India 2016.' New Delhi: Ministry of Statistics and Programme Implementation, Government of India, http://mospi.nic.in/sites/default/files/publication_reports/ElderlyinIndia_2016.pdf.
80. Confederation of Indian Industry, 'CII—Senior Care Industry Report India 2018: Igniting Potential in Senior Care Services.' https://www.slideshare.net/saileshmishra1/cii-senior-care-industry-report-india-2018.
81. 'World Bank Country and Lending Groups.' Washington D.C. World Bank
82. Confederation of Indian Industry, 'CII—Senior Care Industry Report India 2018: Igniting Potential in Senior Care Services.'

The Economy—Moving Towards a Distributed Growth Model

83. '15 Shocking Facts about Inequality in India.' New Delhi: Oxfam India, January 2018, https://www.oxfamindia.org/press-release/6229
84. 'The India 2018 Wealth Report.' Dublin: Research and Markets, June 2018, https://www.researchandmarkets.com/reports/4580166/the-india-2018-wealth-report.
85. Ibid.
86. Ibid.
87. Ibid.

88. Ibid.
89. Krishnan, Sandhya, Neeraj Hatekar, 'Rise of the New Middle Class in India and Its Changing Structure.' *Economic&Political Weekly* vol. 52, issue 22, June 2017, ttps://www.epw.in/author/neeraj-hatekar.
90. 'ATM & Card Statistics for August—2018,' https://rbidocs.rbi.org.in/rdocs/ATM/PDFs/ATMC0820187FB940DB7996455284154AEE2E84D43D.PDF.
91. http://pib.nic.in/newsite/PrintRelease.aspx?relid=181634
92. 'Issue of Kisan Credit Cards.' New Delhi: Press Information Bureau, Government of India, August 2018, http://pib.nic.in/newsite/PrintRelease.aspx?relid=181634.
93. Hae, Kim, 'The Effect of Consumption on Economic Growth in Asia.' *Journal of Global Economics* 2017, vol. 5, issue 3, https://www.omicsonline.org/open-access/the-effect-of-consumption-on-economic-growth-in-asia-2375-4389-1000259.pdf.
94. 'FDI Inflow: India at No. 10.' *The Economic Times*, 22 January 2019, https://epaper.timesgroup.com/Olive/ODN/TheEconomicTimes/shared/ShowArticle.
95. 'German Mittelstand: Engine of the German Economy.' Berlin: Federal Ministry of Economics and Technology.
96. 'Tax Rates.' Income Tax Department, Government of India, 2018, https://bit.ly/2SaTRAj.
97. 'Budget at a Glance 2019–2020.' Income Tax Department, Government of India, 2019, https://www.indiabudget.gov.in/ub2019-20/bag/bag1.pdf.
98. 'Parliament Passes Bill to Punish Bribe Givers, Along with Takers: Highlights.' The Times of India, June 2018, https://bit.ly/2Ijx7Oz.
99. Mishra, Digbijay, '1 in 5 Products Sold by E-tailers Is Fake: Survey.' The Times of India, 11 May 2018, https://bit.ly/2GyTxtt.
100. 'The Convention on the Protection and Promotion of the Diversity of Cultural Expressions.' UNESCO, https://en.unesco.org/creativity/convention.

Correspondences Which Show That Your Inputs Are Never in Vain

VIKSIT BHARAT FOUNDATION

16th July 2003

To
Sri Rajendra,
Vice President,
Medicine Shoppe India,
A/2, Jitendra Estate, Andheri, Kurla Road,
Andheri (E),
Mumbai – 400 093.

Dear Sir,

Further to your discussions with the H.E. The President of India, I am directed to forward a copy of the Registered Trust Deed of Viksit Bharat Foundation which is herewith enclosed.

I am also enclosing a copy of the minutes of the last meeting of the Trust for your kind perusal and the needful.

Thanking you,

Yours sincerely,

(P.S.R.SWAMI)

Encl : As above

Correspondence with Viksit Bharat Foundation

DR MURLI MANOHAR JOSHI
Member of Parliament (Rajya Sabha)
CHAIRMAN
Parliamentary Standing Committee
on Commerce

सत्यमेव जयते

123, Parliament House Annexe
New Delhi-110 001
Tel. : 23034123, 23011991

August 18, 2006

Dear Shri Gupta,

A copy of your letter addressed to Shri Chidambaramji is on my table. You have raised some very important points which need a very careful analysis. Your concern regarding India being several years behind China should be taken seriously.

In my opinion many political leaders in India are directionless and without vision. Their main aim is to get somehow elected to various offices without a clear cut concept about the future of Indian economy, food and geopolitical security and the conditions of the common man. In all my budget speeches I have always raised this question that where is the common man or poor man in this budget. I am happy that you have raised the same issue. Please continue to send you views to me.

With best wishes,

Yours sincerely,

(Murli Manohar Joshi)

Shri Rajendra P. Gupta,
A-101, Devrishi, Plot No.6,
Sector 4, New Panvel-East,
Navi Mumbai-410206

Response from Dr Murli Mahohar Joshi, MP (Rajya Sabha)

सत्यमेव जयते

CHIEF MINISTER OFFICE

TEL. NO. 2339269...
2339269...
FAX NO. 2339211...

CM/PG/VIP/2010/ 466
Dated 16-2-2010

GOVT. OF NATIONAL CAPITAL
TERRITORY OF DELHI
DELHI SECRETARIAT, I.P. ESTAT...
NEW DELHI-110113

Please find enclosed letter dated 24.1.2010 from Sh. Rajendra Pratap Gupta, R/o 102, Siddhivnayak, Plot No.3, Sector-14, Khanda Colony, New Panvel, Navi Mumbai regarding healthcare reforms.

The reference is being forwarded for consideration and appropriate necessary action. The applicant may be informed accordingly under intimation to this office.

(ALKA DIWAN) I.A.S.
Addl. Secretary to C.M.

Secretary to Hon'ble Minister of Health

Copy to Sh. Rajendra Pratap Gupta, R/o 102, Siddhivnayak, Plot No.3, Sector-14, Khanda Colony, New Panvel, Navi Mumbai with the request to contact the concerned department.

(ASHWINI KUMAR)
Superintendent (G)

Letter from the Chief Minister's Office, Government of Delhi

छत्तीसगढ़ शासन
स्वास्थ्य एवं परिवार कल्याण विभाग
दाऊ कल्याण सिंह भवन, मंत्रालय, रायपुर, छत्तीसगढ़

कमांक–स्वा.प.क. /2010/........................ रायपुर, दिनांक /06/2010

प्रति,

श्री के.के. बक्शी,
विशेष कर्तव्यस्थ अधिकारी,
मुख्यमंत्री निवास कार्यालय,
रायपुर, छत्तीसढ़

विषय :– Regarding Healthcare reforms in State ।
संदर्भ :– आपका पत्र कमांक 500710000297/मु.मं.नि./2010 दिनांक 04.02.2010 ।

//0//

विषयांतर्गत संदर्भित पत्र के माध्यम से श्री राजेन्द्र प्रताप गुप्ता द्वारा माननीय मुख्यमंत्री, छत्तीसगढ शासन को संबोधित पत्र में स्वास्थ्य क्षेत्र में सुधार हेतु सुझाव दिया गया है। जिस पर आपके द्वारा आवश्यक कार्यवाही किये जाने हेतु निर्देशित किया गया है।

श्री राजेन्द्र प्रताप गुप्ता द्वारा उपलब्ध कराई गई पुस्तिका का अवलोकन एवं परीक्षण पश्चात् पुस्तक स्वास्थ्य क्षेत्र में सुधार हेतु अत्यंत उपयोगी है, भविष्य में उक्त पुस्तिका में वर्णित जानकारी अनुसार छत्तीसगढ़ राज्य में स्वास्थ्य क्षेत्रों में सुधार हेतु तैयार किये जाने वाली कार्ययोजना में समावेश किया जावेगा।

वर्तमान में छत्तीसगढ़ राज्य में स्वास्थ्य क्षेत्रों में किये जा रहे कार्य का संक्षिप्त विवरण संलग्न प्रेषित है।

संलग्नः– उपरोक्तानुसार (07 पेज)

(विकासशील)
सचिव
छत्तीसगढ़ शासन,
स्वास्थ्य एवं परिवार कल्याण विभाग

पृ0 कमांक–स्वा.प.क./2010/(HSB23)/13/89/Infm/889 रायपुर, दिनांक 19/08/2010
प्रतिलिपिः–

1. श्री राजेन्द्र प्रसाद गुप्ता, 102, सिद्विविनायक, प्लाट–3, से.–14 खण्डा कालानी, न्यू पनवेल (वेस्ट) नवी मुम्बई, महाराष्ट्र
2. संचालक, स्वास्थ्य सेवायें, स्वास्थ्य एवं परिवार कल्याण विभाग रायपुर ।
3. संयुक्त संचालक, राष्ट्रीय ग्रामीण स्वास्थ्य मिशन कार्यकम, रायपुर ।
4. कार्यालयीन प्रति ।

सचिव
छत्तीसगढ़ शासन,
स्वास्थ्य एवं परिवार कल्याण विभाग

D:\javed\secretary\Letter 4 secretary 2009 - Hindi.doc

Letter from the Secretary, Health and Family Welfare, Government of Chhattisgarh

From: S. [mailto:s.hameed@nic.in]
Sent: 18 March 2010 13:13
To: Rajendra P. Gupta / Office G /
Subject: Re: Meeting with Aspen Institute—USA, today

Dear Mr. Gupta,

Thank you for your email and your note on Healthcare. I found your note to be very useful with interesting points about mental health, geriatrics and telehealth. I suggest that you keep in touch with us for future involvement on health sector.

Yours sincerely,
Syeda Hameed

From: XXX
Sent: Wednesday, January 05, 2011 5:52 PM
To: office@rajendragupta.org
Subject: Ref: Your presentation to Dr. Syeda Hameed, Member, Planning Commission on Health Care Reforms, Innovation and Entrepreneurship

Dear Sir

This is in reference to your presentation on Health Care Reforms, Innovation and Entrepreneurship, that you had shared with Dr. Hameed in June. Dr. Hameed appreciated your presentation and had shared it with Sr. Advisor, Health, Dr. Sethi and other Division members.

In this context, Dr. Hameed would appreciate if you could share your views on (1) eradicating under-nutrition and malnutrition in India through restructuring of ICDS or other means and (2) provide pointed suggestions for improvement in the present structure of NRHM.

Your inputs will help planners in writing of the 12th Five Year Plan.

Look forward to interacting with you.

With sincere regards
XXX
Consultant to Dr. Hameed
Planning Commission

Email Exchanges with Member, Planning Commission, Government of India

भारत सरकार
योजना आयोग
योजना भवन
नई दिल्ली-110 001

सत्यमेव जयते

जय हिन्द

Dr. RAKESH SARWAL
Advisor (Health)
Tele No. 23096722

GOVERNMENT OF INDIA
PLANNING COMMISSION
YOJANA BHAWAN
NEW DELHI-110 001

D.O.No. 2(18)/2011-H&FW (Part-III) **Dated : 16th October, 2012**

Dear Shri Rajendra,

This is to acknowledge the receipt of your letter dated 21st August, 2012 to the Prime Minister on "Faster, Sustainable & more inclusive Growth-An approach to the 12th Five Year Plan-Health".

We appreciate your keen interest in issues relating to health, and the suggestions made on the approach towards the 12th Five Year Plan-Health.

I would like to assure you that the Planning Commission fully appreciates and shares your concern on the need for private sector engagement in the healthcare sector and the importance of the role of technology in the health sector. These issues are being examined.

With regards,

Yours sincerely,

16.10.12

(Dr. Rakesh Sarwal)

Shri Rajendra Pratap Gupta
President & Member Board of Directors,
Disaster Management Association of India
102, Siddhivinayak, Plot No. 3, Sector-14,
Khanda Colony,
New Panvel-West,
Navi Mumbai-410206
Maharashtra.

Letter from the Advisor, Health, Planning Commission, Government of India

सत्यमेव जयते

श्रीपाद नाईक
SHRIPAD NAIK

राज्य मंत्री (स्वतंत्र प्रभार)
आयुर्वेद, योग व प्राकृतिक चिकित्सा, यूनानी सिद्ध एवं
होम्योपैथी (आयुष) एवं
राज्य मंत्री (स्वास्थ्य और परिवार कल्याण)
भारत सरकार

**MINISTER OF STATE (INDEPENDENT CHARGE) FOR
AYURVEDA, YOGA & NATUROPATHY
UNANI, SIDDHA AND HOMOEOPATHY (AYUSH)
AND MINISTER OF STATE FOR HEALTH & FAMILY WELFARE
GOVERNMENT OF INDIA**

D.O. No. 131425/**2015**
05 November, 2015

Dear Shri Rajendraji,

It is nice to know that years of your sincere work in the field of Healthcare Reforms will fructify in the form of a well timed book. Your book is a compendium on Healthcare and I must say, "this is a seminal treatise on healthcare, based on exhaustive research. The book has covered extensively various aspects of healthcare and is akin to a data bank of Indian Healthcare! Revealing facts and intriguing insights make it unique to its core. It's thought- provoking, inspiring and simply an incredible work. Congrats ! "

I wish you all the best

Yours sincerely,

[Shripad Naik]

Shri Rajendra Pratap Gupta,
102, Siddhivinayak,
Plot – 3, Sector-14,
Khanda Colony, New Panvel-West,
Navi Mumbai – 410206.

Office : 101, AYUSH Bhavan, 'B' Block, GPO Complex, INA,
New Delhi-110023
Tel : 011-24651955, 011-24651935 Fax : 011-24651936
Office : 250, 'A' Wing, Nirman Bhavan, New Delhi-110 011
Tel. : 011-23061016, 011-23061551 Fax : 011-3061157 Telefax : 23062828
E-mail : shripad.naik@sansad.nic.in

Res (Delhi) : 1, Lodhi Estate, New Delhi-110 003. Tel. : 011-24635396, 011-24641398
Res. (Goa) : "Vijayshree" House No. 111 St. Pedro, Oldgoa, Goa-403402
Tel. :0832-2444510 Fax : 0832-244088

Letter from the Union Minister of State for AYUSH (independent charge) and Minister of State for Health and Family Welfare, Government of India

On Mon, Jun 13, 2016 at 4:35 PM, Rajendra P. Gupta wrote:

Dear Mr. XXXXXXXXX,

Good afternoon

I am sure this finds you doing good, family too.

Wondering if there was any movement / progress on our discussions?

With best regards
Rajendra

From: 'xxxxxxxx'
Subject: Re: Test Email
Date: June 14, 2016 at 3:46:32 PM GMT+5:30
To: 'Rajendra P. Gupta'

Dear Mr. Gupta,

Thank you for your Email. I had circulated your note to the various functionaries concerned. I will have to check on the status.

I am aware that your points on Railways have been / are being substantially implemented--food charges on Rajdhani, trying to do away with waitlist by adding duplicate train, while others are being implemented or under serious consideration (promoting use of stations/ platforms, more emphasis on advertising) etc. From memory, I also recall your suggestions on spiral bound books in schools to reduce load, tailors in Khadi shops, scaling up Jan Aushadhi but do not know the status of implementation. I will check.

Regards,
XXXXXXXXX

Email Correspondence with a Senior Official in the Prime Minister's Office

-------- Original Message --------
From: 'Mission Mudra'
Date: Nov 15, 2016 12:42:10 PM
Subject: Scheme for loans to drivers of taxis attached to mobile/app based cab services like Ola, Uber etc.
To: Rajendra Pratap Gupta
Cc: Navnit, rajiv.s

Sir,

Please refer to your suggestions on the captioned subject and find attached our comments in the matter.

Regards

Mission Mudra
Pradhan Mantri Mudra Yojana (PMMY)
Department of Financial Services
Ministry of Finance
New Delhi

<u>Correspondence with the Ministry of Finance, Government of India (See following pages)</u>

e-mail

F.NO.10/25/2016-IF-II
Government of India
Ministry of Finance
Department of Financial Services
****

Jeevan Deep Building, Sansad Marg, New Delhi,
Dated the 11th November, 2016

To

Sh. Rajendra Pratap Gupta

Subject: Scheme for loans to drivers of taxis attached to mobile/app based cab services like Ola, Uber etc.

Sir,

Please refer to suggestions made by you on the above noted subject to the Prime Minister's Office (PMO). The suggestions have been examined and the undersigned has been directed to inform that collateral free loans upto Rs.10 lakhs under Pradhan Mantri Mudra Yojana (PMMY) are available for Service Sector. Since plying of taxis come under this Sector, loans to prospective borrowers are already available under PMMY from various banks. Some instances are indicated below.

2. Under PMMY, Bank of Baroda has developed a new sub-product namely Vehicle finance Product for drivers and Vehicle Service providers under tie up arrangement with Taxi Aggregators with maximum limit of Rs.10 lakhs per vehicle in case of driver borrower. In case of Service providers like Tour operators/Taxi service providers, a separate limit is envisaged. These loans are collateral free loans. Bank is desirous of entering into tie-up arrangement with aggregators such as UBER for financing on board drivers of Uber for purchase of vehicle. Similarly, Punjab National Bank has taken up financing of e-rickshaws through 'PNB Green Ride'. A large number of units have been financed in Delhi to begin with. E-rickshaws are now on an Ola app.

3. State Bank of India has rolled out a tie-up with various taxi aggregators & hybrid model operators (e.g. OLA, Uber, Ecorentacar etc.) across selected cities for vehicle finance to driver entrepreneurs under PMMY. Vijaya Bank has entered in to MOU with OLA Cab' on 31.08.2016 for financing cabs to unemployed drivers and transport operators to be engaged with the cab aggregator. Ola Cab will identify the eligible

Contd...2/-

drivers/transport operators who intend to engage their Cab with them and forward the loan proposal to the Bank along with KYC/ other related documents. Dena Bank is in process of tie up arrangement with Ola cabs for providing financial assistance to Drivers/taxi owners for purchase of vehicles under PMMY.

4. IDBI Bank has entered into a MoU with OLA Cab for financing "probable passenger transport service providers" to enable them to purchase passenger vehicles for providing transport services, under the brand OLA CAB. The have also entered into MoUs/Tie-ups with renowned Automobile Manufacturers viz. i) Bajaj Auto Ltd., ii) TVS Motors Ltd., iii) Tata Motors Ltd., iv) Auto Auto Ltd., v) Saera Auto Electric Pvt. Ltd., vi) Maruti Udyog Ltd., etc.

5. It is also pertinent to mention here that Department of Rural Development has circulated a draft Scheme titled "Pradhan Mantri Gram Parivahan Yojana (PMGPY)". The Scheme proposes to provide vehicular access to villages with population more than 10000 by providing for a one time assistance to transport service operator in the form of Viability Gap Funding (VGF) meant for meeting the cost of the vehicle in addition to admissibility under the Tarun Loan Category of PMMY which is from Rs.5 lakhs to Rs.10 lacs. A provision of a one time financial assistance upto Rs.4.00 lakhs or 50% of the vehicle cost, whichever is lower has been proposed per beneficiary, under this scheme. In the first year, 8095 vehicles are proposed to be financed under PMMY.

6. Mudra Ltd. is a refinancing institution and does not extend loans directly. It refinances banks & MFIs which give PMMY loans, as indicated above.

7. I hope the above details clarifies the position.

Yours faithfully,

Director (IF-2)

Tele.

e-mail :

Copy to : - Joint Secretary to PM, Prime Minister's Office with reference to .1 dated the 28th October, 2016.

खादी और ग्रामोद्योग आयोग
KHADI AND VILLAGE
INDUSTRIES COMMISSION
सूक्ष्म, लघु और मध्यम उद्यम मंत्रालय, भारत सरकार
Ministry of Micro, Small & Medium Enterprises, Govt. of India.
DIRECTORATE OF MARKETING/GOVT.SUPPLY

No. MKT/Min-VIP Ref/2015-16/857 Date:- 24.2.2016

To,
Sh. J.K.Sahu,
Under Secretary,
Ministry of MSME,
Udyog Bhavan,
Govt of India,
New Delhi-110011.

Sub: Reference received from Shri Rajendra P. Gupta, enclosing suggestions for implementation at sales outlet level reg.

Ref:- Letter no. A-54/13/2016-KVI-P dated 1/02/2016.

Sir,

This office is in receipt of your letter as referred above along with the suggestions of Shri Rajendra P. Gupta, for implementation at the sales outlet level.

The suggestions are well taken and being transmitted to the departmental sales outlet as well as sales outlet run by institutions. The information is being given to Shri Rajendra P. Gupta, through email.

This is issued with the approval of CEO.

Yours faithfully,

Dy. Director I/C (Marketing)

Copy to:-

(1)The Director (EcR), KVIC, Mumbai-56 for information please.
(2) Shri Rajendra P.Gupta for information . E-mail:-office.rajendra@gmail.com

R. Narayan

for Dy. Director I/C (Marketing)

ग्रामोदय, 3, इर्ला रोड, विले पार्ले (प.), मुंबई -56
Gramodaya, 3, Irla Road, Vile Parle (W), Mumbai- 56
Tel: 022- 2671 6680 /4320 /4322, 022-26713528 /29
Fax: 022-2624 1738, E-mail: marketing@kvic.gov.in

Letter from the Khadi and Village Industries Commission, Ministry of MSME, Government of India

By Speed post

भारतीय संसद

PARLIAMENT OF INDIA

राज्य सभा सचिवालय

RAJYA SABHA SECRETARIAT

संसद भवन/संसदीय सौध,
नई दिल्ली-110001
वेबसाइट : http://rajyasabhahindi.nic.in

Parliament House / Annexe,
New Delhi-110001
Website : http://rajyasabha.nic.in

R.S.5/1/2018-Com. (H&FW) **Dated 9th February, 2018**

From

DINESH SINGH
ADDITIONAL DIRECTOR

To

Shri Rajendra Pratap Gupta,
Chairman, Personal Connected Health Alliance,
102, Siddhivinayak Plot – 3, Sector – 14,
Khanda, New Panvel, Mumbai - 410206,

Sub: - The National Medical Commission Bill, 2017-reg.

Sir,

I am directed to state that the Department-related Parliamentary Standing Committee on Health and Family Welfare is presently examining the National Medical Commission Bill, 2017. In this connection, the Committee has decided to seek your views on the various provisions of the Bill. A copy of the Bill is enclosed.

2. I am, therefore, to request you kindly to arrange to furnish the views/ comments/suggestions (alongwith soft copy) of your association on various provisions of the Bill **latest by 20th February, 2018** for consideration of the Committee.

Yours faithfully,

(DINESH SINGH)
Tel: 011- 23035581 (O)
Fax:011-23094298
E-mail:-rs-chfw@sansad.nic.in

Letter from the Parliamentary Standing Committee on Health and Family Welfare, Government of India

13/4/19

April

(R)

207 dt. 13/4/19